Anonymous

Constitution and Playing Rules of the National League of Professional Base Ball Clubs

Anonymous

Constitution and Playing Rules of the National League of Professional Base Ball Clubs

ISBN/EAN: 9783337885823

Printed in Europe, USA, Canada, Australia, Japan

Cover: Foto ©Andreas Hilbeck / pixelio.de

More available books at **www.hansebooks.com**

1877.

CONSTITUTION

AND

PLAYING ·RULES

OF THE

NATIONAL LEAGUE

OF

Professional Base Ball Clubs.

OFFICIAL PUBLICATION,

Including the Proceedings of the League Congress in Cleveland, Dec. 6-8, 1876, and the Official Fielding and Batting Averages of Players in Championship Games in 1876.

CHICAGO:

PUBLISHED BY A. G. SPALDING & BRO.,

NO. 118 RANDOLPH STREET.

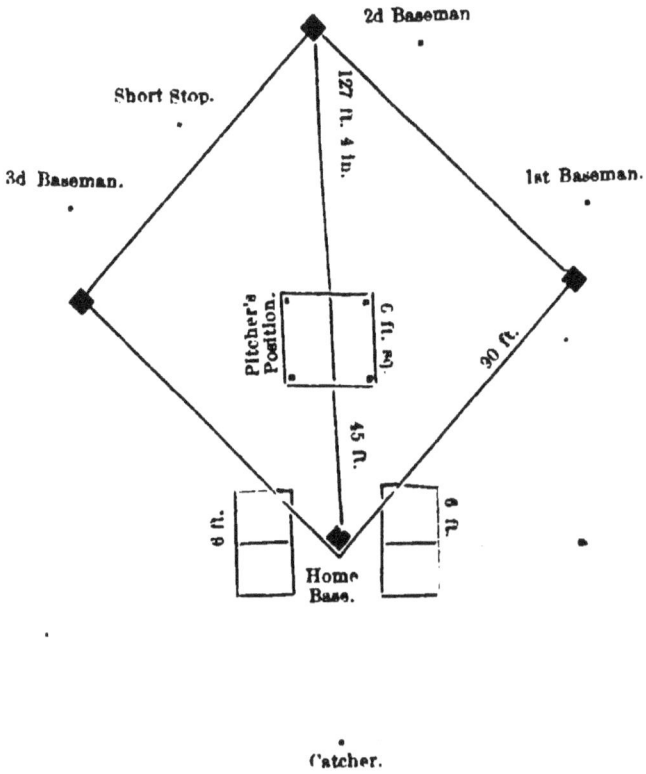

Center Field

Left Field.

Right Field.

2d Baseman

Short Stop.

3d Baseman.

1st Baseman.

127 ft. 4 in.

Pitcher's Position.

6 ft. sq.

30 ft.

45 ft.

6 ft.

6 ft.

Home Base.

Catcher.

CONSTITUTION

OF THE

NATIONAL LEAGUE

-OF

PROFESSIONAL BASE BALL CLUBS.

1877.

ARTICLE I.

NAME.

This Association shall be called "THE Name. NATIONAL LEAGUE OF PROFESSIONAL BASE BALL CLUBS."

ARTICLE II.

OBJECTS.

The objects of this League are:

1st. To encourage, foster, and elevate the Objects. game of base ball; to enact and enforce proper rules for the exhibition and conduct of the game, and to make base ball playing respectable and honorable.

2d. To protect and promote the mutual interests of professional base ball clubs and professional base ball players; and

3d. To establish and regulate the base ball championship of the United States.

ARTICLE III.

MEMBERSHIP.

This League shall consist of the following named Professional Base Ball Clubs, namely:

Boston B. B. Club, of Boston, Mass.
Chicago B. B. Club, of Chicago, Ill.
Cincinnati B. B. Club, of Cincinnati, O.
Hartford B. B. Club, of Hartford, Conn.
Louisville B. B. Club, of Louisville, Ky.
St. Louis B. B. Club, of St. Louis, Mo.

And such other professional base ball clubs as may from time to time be elected to membership under the following rules, namely:

1. No club shall be admitted from either of the cities above named other than the clubs mentioned, except in the event that either of such clubs shall lose its membership, and in no event shall there be more than one club from any city.

2. No club shall be admitted from any city whose population is less than seventy-five thousand (75,000), except by unanimous vote of the League.

3. No club shall be admitted unless it shall first have delivered to the Secretary of the League, at least five days before the annual meeting, a written application for membership, signed by its President and Secretary, accompanied by documents showing that such club bears the name of the city in which it is located, and that it is regularly organized and officered and (where the State law permits it) chartered, and accompanied also by a pledge that it will keep all its engagements with the clubs members of the League, and that it has not in its employ any player who has been dismissed or expelled by the League or any club member

thereof; and the Secretary shall refer such application to the Board at its annual meeting.

4. The voting upon an application for membership shall be by white and black balls. Two black balls shall be sufficient to exclude the applicant, and no club shall be required, under any circumstances, to state how it voted upon such application. Such election shall take place at the annual meeting of the League; provided, that should any eligible club desire to join the League after the adjournment of the annual meeting and before the commencement of the ensuing championship season, it may make application in writing to the Secretary of the League, who shall at once communicate such application, together with any facts in his possession concerning such applicant, to all League clubs, each of whom shall, within ten days, transmit one written ballot for or against the admission of such applicant to the Secretary, and if two adverse ballots be not cast, then the Secretary shall, upon receipt of the annual dues, notify such club of its election.

ARTICLE IV.

OFFICERS.

SECTION 1. The affairs of this League shall Officers. be conducted and controlled by five Directors, who shall constitute "The Board," who shall Board. hold their office for one year, and shall be chosen at the annual meeting in the following manner: The name of each club shall be plainly How chosen. written upon a card—in full view of the delegates present—by the Secretary; the cards to be of the same size, shape, color and material. The cards shall then be placed in some suitable receptacle and well shaken together; thereupon five of these cards shall be drawn successively and at random, and one delegate from each of the five clubs whose names are so drawn shall compose the Board, and if any club whose name is thus drawn be represented by two delegates, such delegation shall name one of its number to be a member of the Board.

Chairman.   SEC. 2.   The Board shall elect a chairman from their number.   He shall preside at all meetings of the Board and discharge the usual duties of such an officer.   In the event of his absence, the Board shall elect a chairman *pro tem.*

Secretary and Treasurer.   SEC. 3.   The Board shall also elect a gentleman of intelligence, honesty and good repute, who is versed in base ball matters, but who is not, in any manner, connected with the press, and who is not a member of any professional base ball club either in or out of the League, to be the Secretary of the Board and of the League.

Treasurer's duties.   The Secretary shall be the Treasurer of the League, and as such shall be the custodian of all the funds of the League, receive all dues, fees and assessments, pay out such sums as he may be directed to do by the Board or by vote of the League, and render annually a report of his accounts.

Secretary's duties.   He shall have the custody and care of the official records and papers of the League; shall keep a true record of all meetings of the League and the Board; shall issue all official notices and attend to the necessary correspondence; he shall prepare and furnish such reports as may be called for by the Board, and shall be entitled to such books, stationery, blanks and materials as the actual duties of his office may require.

He shall receive such salary as the League, Salary. by vote, shall determine, which salary shall not be less than three hundred dollars ($300) nor more than five hundred dollars ($500) per annum, and shall be reimbursed for all traveling expenses actually incurred by him in the service of the League; and the Board may exact from him such guarantees for the faith- Guarantee. ful performance of his duties as they may deem for the interest and safety of the League.

At the expiration of his term of office, he shall account for and deliver up to the Board all the property and papers which may have come into his hands by virtue of his office.

SEC. 4. In case of a vacancy in the Board Vacancy in by reason of the death, resignation, absence, the Board. or disqualification of any director, the club of which he was a member at the time he was chosen shall designate his successor, and at once notify the Secretary. But if such vacancy is caused by the withdrawal, disbanding or disqualification of a club represented on the Board, the Board may fill the vacancy by election in the same manner as provided for the election of Directors in Article IV, Section 1, of this Constitution.

No person shall be qualified to act as a direct- Directors' or who is not an actual member of the club he qualifica- represents; nor shall any club, under any cir- tions. cumstances, be represented by more than one person on the Board.

SEC. 5. The Board shall have the general Board's supervision and management of all the affairs duties. and business of the League, and shall be individually answerable to the League for the faithful discharge of their trust.

The Board shall meet annually on the even- Annual ing of the first Tuesday in December, at the Meeting of Board and Report.

place where the annual meeting of the League is to be held, but may hold special meetings whenever urgent necessity may require. They shall prepare a detailed report of all their doings, and present the same in writing to the League at its annual meeting, which report shall, if accepted, be filed with the Secretary, together with all official papers, documents and property which may have come into their possession by virtue of their office.

Penalty. Any director who shall disclose or publish any of the proceedings of the Board, except officially through the report of the Board, or when called upon by vote of the League, shall forfeit his office.

ARTICLE V.

CLUBS.

Clubs. SECTION 1. Each club belonging to this League shall have the right to regulate its own affairs, to make its own contracts, to establish its own rules, and to discipline and punish its own players: *Provided*, That nothing shall be done in violation of, or contrary to, this Constitution or the Playing Rules.

Employment of Expelled Players forbidden. SEC. 2. No club shall employ as manager, scorer or player any person who has willfully violated any provision of this Constitution or of the Playing Rules, or who has been discharged, dismissed or expelled from any club belonging to this League, or who shall be disqualified from playing with a club under any provision of this Constitution; and any club which shall employ or play, or attempt to play, in its nine in any championship game, a player disqualified by any provision of this Constitution, shall at once forfeit its membership in the League, and all other clubs must and shall, under penalty of the forfeiture of their membership in the League, abstain from playing any such club until it shall have been reinstated or reelected to membership.

SEC. 3. Any club having agreed to play with another club upon a day certain, and refusing or failing to meet its engagement, shall (unless the failure be caused by an unavoidable accident in traveling, or the game be prevented by rain or postponed with the consent, in writing, of the other club) at once forfeit its membership in the League, and all other League clubs must and shall, under penalty of the forfeiture of their membership in the League, abstain from playing any such club until it shall have been reinstated or reelected to membership.

SEC. 4. In any case subject to the provisions of Sections 2 or 3 of this Article, the club not in default shall at once notify the Secretary of the League by writing or telegraph of the default of the other club, stating the particulars of such default, and upon the receipt of such notice the Secretary shall at once notify all League clubs, and the club in default, of the forfeiture of membership of such club, stating in such notice the nature of the default, and referring to the Section of this Article under which such forfeiture of membership was incurred.

SEC. 5. Every club member of this League Territory. shall have exclusive control of the city in which it is located, and of the territory surrounding such city to the extent of five miles in every direction, and no visiting League club shall, under any circumstances—not even with the consent of the local League club, until all

League games on that ground shall have been finished—be allowed to play any club in such territory other than the League club therein located.

Member-ship. SEC. 6. The players and managers employed by the clubs belonging to this League shall be considered and treated as members hereof to the extent of being always amenable to the provisions of this Constitution, and entitled to all its privileges in matters of dispute, grievance or discipline, as provided in this Constitution.

ARTICLE VI.

DUES AND ASSESSMENTS.

Dues. SECTION 1. Every club shall pay to the Secretary of the League, on or before the first day of June of each year, the sum of One Hundred Dollars as annual dues, and any club failing to pay said sum by such time shall thereby forfeit its membership in the League, and the Secretary of the League shall at once notify all League clubs of such forfeiture of membership.

Assessments. SEC. 2. In case of necessity thereof, the Board may levy a pro rata assessment upon the clubs, to be paid as the Board may direct.

ARTICLE VII.

FORFEITING MEMBERSHIP.

Forfeiting Membership The membership of any club belonging to this League shall be forfeited under the following circumstances, namely:

1st. By voluntary withdrawal or disbandment.

2d. By failing or refusing to comply with any lawful requirement or order of the Board.

By willfully violating any provision of this Constitution, or the Playing Rules adopted hereunder: *Provided*, That in all cases where this Constitution does not specifically inflict immediate forfeiture of membership, such forfeiture shall be subject to a two-thirds vote of the League at its annual meeting, and no club which has forfeited its membership shall be readmitted except by unanimous vote of the League.

ARTICLE VIII.

DISPUTES AND COMPLAINTS.

SECTION 1. The Board of Directors shall at once consider any complaint preferred by a club against a player of another club for conduct in violation of any provision of this Constitution or prejudicial to the good repute of the game of base ball, and shall have power to require the club to which such player may belong to discipline him, and, upon repetition of such offense, to expel him: *Provided*, That such complaint be preferred in writing, giving such particulars as may enable the Board to ascertain all the facts, and be transmitted to the Secretary, by whom it shall at once be referred to the Board.

SEC. 2. The Board shall be the sole tribunal to determine disputes between two or more clubs which involve the interpretation or construction of this Constitution, or any of its Articles, and facts in controversy, or any question of fact arising thereunder. When such a dispute arises, and either club shall signify to the other its desire for the Board to decide the matter, each club shall furnish to the Secretary, as soon as possible, a written statement of its side of the dispute, with the names of its witnesses, or an agreed statement of facts, if possible, which the Secretary shall docket in the order of its reception, and at the next annual meeting the clubs shall present themselves before the Board with their testimony, and the Board shall proceed to try the case impartially and render a true verdict. The Board shall have a right to put the witnesses under oath, and must do so if demanded thereto by either party. No director shall sit on the trial of a cause in which his club is interested, but must retire and permit the others alone to determine the matter. The finding of the Board, in such a case, shall be *final*, and under no circumstances shall be reconsidered, reopened or inquired into, either by the League or any subsequent Board; *Provided*, That in case the matter in dispute shall involve the forfeiture of membership of a League club during the playing season, the Board shall, if appealed to by such club through the Secretary of the League, forthwith determine the matter, but, in such case, the members of the Board shall (unless the ends of justice may seem to them to require a meeting) determine such question by conference with each other by written correspondence.

Player's appeal from his club. SEC. 3. The Board shall also be the sole tribunal for the hearing of an appeal made by any player who shall have been dismissed, expelled or otherwise disciplined by his club, or for an alleged breach of contract. The matter shall be proceeded with in the following manner: The player shall file with the Secretary an affidavit signed by himself, in which he shall deny, under oath, that he is guilty of the offense for which he has been disciplined, accompanied by a request that an appeal be allowed

him. The Secretary shall notify the club of
the affidavit and request for appeal, and at the
next annual meeting the club and the player
shall appear before the Board with their testimony. The Board shall impartially hear the
matter and render their decision, which shall
be *final* and forever binding on both club and
player. In the event the club appealed from
is represented in the Board, that representative
shall not be allowed to sit in the matter.

SEC. 4. All differences and disputes arising ^{Disputes}
between clubs in which the interpretation, con- concerning Playing
struction or violation of the Playing Rules is Rules.
involved shall be adjusted in the following
manner: The complaining club shall file a Arbitrators
written statement of its grievance, accompanied with the affidavits of its witnesses, with
the Secretary, who (unless the other club has
also filed its statement and affidavits, or an
agreed case has been prepared) shall immediately notify the defendant club of the fact
that a complaint—briefly stating the nature
thereof—has been filed with him, and call for a
counter statement with affidavits, which must
be furnished to him within fifteen (15) days
of the date of the notice. On receiving the
counter statement, or agreed case, or in the
event the defendant club does not comply with
the call within fifteen (15) days, the Secretary
shall notify the President of the matter, who
shall appoint three disinterested persons, members of League clubs, as arbitrators, to the first
of whom the Secretary shall transmit at once
all the papers in the case, securely sealed, noti-
fying him of the remaining arbitrators. Within
three days, such person shall attach his verdict
in writing to the papers and transmit them to
the second person, who shall within three days

attach his written verdict and transmit them to the third, who, following the rule, shall finally return them to the Secretary, and he shall at once notify each club of the finding. A majority of the arbitrators shall determine the cause, and from their finding there shall be no appeal.

Expenses The expense of all trials and arbitrations shall be equally borne by the parties litigant.

ARTICLE IX.

ANNUAL MEETING.

Annual meeting. SECTION 1. The annual meeting of the League shall be held on the first Wednesday after the first Tuesday in December of each year, at twelve o'clock noon, and at such place as shall be determined by vote at the previous annual meeting. The annual meeting shall not be held in any city where a club member of the League is located; but shall be held in some easily accessible place, and, as near as may be, equidistant from the several club members.

SEC. 2. At such meeting each club shall be entitled to two representatives, who shall present a certificate from the President or Secretary of their club, showing their authority to act; but no club shall have more than one vote.

Quorum. A representation of a majority of clubs shall constitute a quorum for the transaction of business, but a less number may adjourn from time to time until a quorum is obtained.

SEC. 3. The following shall be the order of business.

1st—Reading minutes of last meeting.
2d—Report of Board of Directors.
3d—Miscellaneous business.
4th—Amendment of Constitution.
5th—Amendment of Playing Rules.

6th—Election of new members.
7th—Election of officers.
8th—Adjournment.

ARTICLE X.

PLAYING RULES.

The League at its first meeting shall adopt a code of Playing Rules, which may be altered, amended or abolished at any subsequent annual meeting.

Playing Rules

ARTICLE XI.

CONTRACTS.

SECTION 1. Contracts hereafter made between the clubs, members of this League, and their players shall be made under and in view of the following provisions:

Contracts.

No club shall be prevented from contracting with a player for the reason that he is already under contract with another club: *Provided,* The service to be rendered under the second contract is not to begin until the expiration of the first contract.

Contracts may be made at any time.

No formal words of contract shall be required. It shall be sufficient if the contract be made in writing, be dated, specify the time, indicate the service, and be signed by the player and some officer or recognized agent of the club and one witness.

No formality necessary.

Requisites of contract

Every contract made after Jan. 1, 1877, shall contain the following stipulations: "It is also agreed by the parties hereto that this contract shall not be valid or binding until the receipt by the Secretary of 'The National League of Professional Base Ball Clubs' of a notification, signed by the parties hereto, of the making of this contract; and it is further agreed that should the club party hereto lose its membership in said 'National League of Professional Base Ball Clubs' at any time before the expiration of the period covered by this contract, then, immediately upon such loss of membership, the mutual contract obligations of the parties hereto shall at once cease and terminate."

Notice to Secretary. SEC. 2. It shall be the duty of a club, as soon as it shall have entered into a contract with a player, to file a notification of the same, stating therein that the provisions of Section 1 of this article have been complied with, and signed by the club and the player, with the Secretary of the League, who shall endorse thereon the date of its reception, and forthwith notify every other League club of such contract, and no contract shall be valid until the receipt of such notice by the Secretary.

Release of players. SEC. 3. Whenever a club releases a player from his contract, that club shall at once notify the Secretary of the League in writing, who shall in turn notify all the other clubs. In case the release shall have been granted for a cause that does not in any manner reflect upon the character of the player, there must be written upon the notice a statement to that effect, otherwise it shall be inferred from such notice that such player has been in fact dismissed, discharged or expelled, and he shall not be eligible to make any contract for the remainder of the season with any League club.

A player who has been released from his contract without imputation may engage with any other club twenty days thereafter.

Expulsion final. No player who has been dismissed or expelled from a League club shall, at any time thereafter, be allowed to play with any League club (either the one expelling him or any other), unless, upon his appeal to the Board, such dismissal or expulsion shall have been set aside.

SEC. 4. A player whose contract has expired or become void by reason of his club's disbanding, withdrawing from or losing its membership in the League, may engage for the remainder of the season with any other League club, provided such engagement shall not commence within twenty days of such disbanding or withdrawal.

ARTICLE XII.

SECTION 1. As a token of good will and friendship for all base ball clubs not members of this League, and with a view of stimulating a proper rivalry among such clubs and of advancing public interest in the game of base ball, it is hereby declared that any club whose organization and conduct are not inconsistent with the objects of this League as expressed in Article II of its Constitution, and which shall have won from other clubs, during an entire playing season, the greatest number of games played under the rules of this League, in series so arranged as to afford a fair test of merit, shall, if otherwise compatible with the Constitution of this League, be eligible to membership in this League at its ensuing annual meeting, provided such club shall, not less than ten days before the annual meeting, make application, in writing, to the Secretary for such membership, accompanying the application with such documentary evidence as may enable the Board of Directors to ascertain whether the provisions of this Article have been complied with ; and it shall be the duty of the Secretary, on receipt of such application and documents, to at once refer them to the Board, who shall examine and report thereon to the League at its annual meeting.

Sec. 2. The Board may, if thereunto requested by other clubs, adjudicate disputes in the manner provided in Article VIII, so far as the provisions of that Article may be applicable thereto; *Provided,* That all communications must be addressed to the Secretary of the League.

Sec. 3. The Secretary of the League may, on application, furnish information to other clubs on matters pertaining to club organization, playing rules and engagements of players by League clubs.

Sec. 4. No club that has forfeited its membership in the League shall be entitled to the benefits of this Article.

Sec. 5. No game of ball shall be played between a League club and any other club employing or presenting in its nine a player expelled from the League.

ARTICLE XIII.

CHAMPIONSHIP.

Championship.   Section 1. The *Championship of the United States,* established by this League, shall be contended for (by the clubs composing this League) under the following rules, namely :

The *championship season* shall extend from the 15th day of March to (and including) the 15th day of November, and no game shall count in the championship series unless played during the championship season.

No game played on Sunday shall count in the championship series.

SEC. 2. Every game played between two clubs from the commencement of the championship season to the completion of the championship series, between such clubs, shall be a game for the championship (unless played on Sunday).

SEC. 3. Each club shall play the following number of games with every other club: If six or seven clubs be members of the League on the first day of the championship season, twelve games; if eight or nine clubs, ten games; if ten clubs, eight games: *Provided, however,* That if any game be prevented by rain, or if a tie or drawn game be played, the visiting club shall not be required to extend its stay, or to again visit such city for the sole purpose of playing off such tie or drawn game, or game prevented by rain.

SEC. 4. Each club shall be entitled to have half of the championship series of games with every other club played on its own grounds.

SEC. 5. All games shall be arranged for in writing, and so as to complete the championship series before the expiration of the championship season. Each agreement to play shall provide for an equal number of return games and specify dates for each game covered by the agreement, which dates shall subsequently be changed only by the written consent of the parties to such agreement.

SEC. 6. A club shall be entitled to forfeited games—to count in its series as games won by a score of nine runs to none—in cases where the umpire in any championship game shall award the game to such club on account of the violation by the contesting club of any playing rule of this League.

SEC. 7. Drawn, tie and postponed games shall not count in the series in favor of either contestant, but may be played off if sufficient time exist before the close of the season.

SEC. 8. The club which shall have won the greatest number of games in the championship series shall be declared the champion club of the United States for the season in which such games were played. In the event two or more clubs shall have won the same number of games, then the club which shall have lost the smallest number shall be declared the champion.

The emblem of the championship shall be a pennant (of the national colors), to cost not less than one hundred dollars ($100). It shall be inscribed with the motto, "Champion Base Ball Club of the United States," with the name of the club and the year in which the title was won ; and the champion club shall be entitled to fly the pennant until the close of the ensuing season.

SEC. 9. The championship shall be decided in the following manner, namely:

Within twenty-four hours after every match game played for the championship, the home club shall prepare and forward to the Secretary of the League, a statement containing the full score of the game, according to the system specified in the "Playing Rules," the date, place where played, and the names of the clubs and umpire : *Provided*, That no tie or drawn game shall be considered "a game" for any purpose, nor shall the score thereof be forwarded to the Secretary.

At the close of the season, the Secretary shall prepare a tabular statement of the games won and lost by each club, according to the statements so sent him (which statements shall be the sole evidence in the matter), and submit the same, with the statements so sent him, to the Board, who shall make the award in writing, and report the same to the League at its annual meeting. In making the award the Board shall consider:

1st. The tabular statement of the Secretary.

2d. Forfeited games.

3d. Games participated in by clubs which have withdrawn, disbanded or forfeited their membership without completing their championship series with all other League clubs; such games shall be counted to the following extent, namely: The Board shall ascertain the least number of championship games played by such club with any club remaining in the League, and shall, from the first games participated in during the championship season, by such retired club, count in the series of each League club a similar number of games, and all other games participated in by such retired club shall not be counted in the championship series: *Provided*, That if such retired club shall have failed to play at least one championship game with every League club, all games participated in by it shall be thrown out entirely.

ARTICLE XIV.

FIELD RULES.

Every club in this League shall be bound by the following Field Rules, and must have the same conspicuously posted or placarded upon its grounds, namely: No club shall allow open betting or pool selling upon its grounds, nor in any building owned or occupied by it. No person shall be allowed upon any part of the field during the progress of a game, in addition to those playing and the umpire, except the managers, scorers and necessary servants of the two clubs, and such officers of the law as may be present to preserve the peace.

Players in uniform shall not be permitted to seat themselves among the spectators.

The umpire is the sole judge of play, and is entitled to the respect of the spectators, and any person hissing or hooting at, or offering any insult or indignity to him, must be promptly ejected from the grounds.

Every club shall furnish sufficient police force upon its own grounds to preserve order, and in the event of a crowd entering the field during the progress of a game, and interfering with the play in any manner, the visiting club may refuse to play further until the field be cleared; and if the ground be not cleared within fifteen minutes thereafter, the visiting club may claim, and shall be entitled, to the game by a score of nine runs to none (no matter what number of innings have been played).

ARTICLE XV.

AMENDMENTS.

Amendments.

This Constitution may be altered or amended by a two-thirds vote of the League at any annual meeting.

PLAYING RULES

OF THE

NATIONAL LEAGUE

OF

PROFESSIONAL BASE BALL CLUBS.

1877.

RULE 1.—THE MATERIALS OF THE GAME.

SECTION 1. The ball must weigh not less *The ball.* than five nor more than five and one-quarter ounces avoirdupois. It must measure not less than nine nor more than nine and one-quarter inches in circumference. It must be composed of woolen yarn, and shall not contain more than one ounce of vulcanized rubber in mould form, and shall be covered with leather, and to be furnished by the Secretary of the League.

SEC. 2. In all games, the ball or balls played *Furnishing the ball.* with shall be furnished by the home club, and shall become the property of the winning club.

SEC. 3. No ball shall be played with in any *A legal ball* championship game unless it is furnished by the Secretary of the League.

SEC. 4. When the ball becomes out of shape, *Changing the ball.* or cut or ripped so as to expose the yarn, or in any way so injured as to be unfit for fair use, a new ball shall be called for by the umpire at the end of an even innings, at the request of either captain. Should the ball be lost during a game, the umpire shall, at the expiration of five minutes, call for a new ball.

Bat. SEC. 5. The bat must be round, and must not exceed two and one-half inches in diameter in the thickest part. It must be made wholly of wood, and shall not exceed forty-two inches in length.

Bases. SEC. 6. The bases must be four in number, and they must be placed and securely fastened upon each corner of a square the sides of which are respectively thirty yards. The bases must be so constructed and placed as to be distinctly seen by the umpire. The first, second and third bases must cover a space equal to fifteen inches square, and the home base one square foot of surface. The first, second and third bases shall be canvas bags, painted white and filled with some soft material. The home base shall be of white marble or stone, so fixed in the ground as to be even with the surface, and wholly within the diamond. One corner of said base shall face the pitcher's position, and two sides shall form part of the foul lines.

Position of the Bases. SEC. 7. The base from which the ball is struck shall be designated the home base, and must be directly opposite the second base. The first base must always be that upon the right hand, and the third base that upon the left hand side of the striker when occupying his position at the home base. In all match games, lines connecting the home and first bases, and the home and third bases, and also the lines of the striker's and pitcher's positions, shall be marked by the use of chalk or other suitable material, so as to be distinctly seen by the umpire. The line of the home base shall extend four feet on each side of the base, and shall be drawn through its center and parallel with a line extending from first to third base. Two lines marked in the same way as the foul lines, and parallel with said foul lines, shall be drawn, one fifteen feet and the other fifty feet distant from them.

RULE II.—THE GAME.

SECTION 1. The game shall consist of nine innings to each side, but should the score then be a tie, play shall be continued until a majority of runs for one side, upon an equal number of innings, shall be declared, when the game shall end. All innings shall be concluded when the third hand is put out.

The Innings

SEC. 2. The home club shall first take the bat. The fielders of each club shall take any position in the field their captain may assign them, with the exception of pitcher, who must deliver the ball from his appointed position.

Position of Players.

SEC. 3. No player taking part in a game shall be replaced by another after the commencement of the second inning, except for reason of illness or injury.

Substitutes.

SEC. 4. No game shall be considered as played unless five innings on each side shall be completed. Should darkness or rain intervene before the third hand is put out in the closing part of the fifth innings of a game, the umpire shall declare "No game."

Five innings necessary.

SEC. 5. Whenever a game of five or more innings is stopped by rain or darkness, and the score at the time is equal on the even innings played, the game shall be declared drawn, but, under no other circumstances, shall a drawn game be declared.

Drawn Games.

SEC. 6. Should rain commence to fall during the progress of a match game, the umpire must

Rain

note the time it began, and should it continue for five minutes, he shall, at the request of either captain, suspend play. Should the rain continue to fall for thirty minutes, after play has been suspended, the game shall terminate.

Calling Play and Time. SEC. 7. When the umpire calls "play," the game must at once be proceeded with. Should either party fail to take their appointed positions in the game, or to commence play as requested, the umpire shall, at the expiration of five minutes, declare the game forfeited by the nine that refuses to play. When the umpire calls "time," play shall be suspended until he call "play" again, and during the interim no player shall be put out, base be run or run be scored. The umpire shall suspend play only for a valid reason, and is not empowered to do so for trivial causes at the request of any player.

Suspending Play. SEC. 8. The umpire, in any match game, shall determine when play shall be suspended, and, if the game cannot be fairly concluded, it shall be decided by the score of the last equal innings played, unless one nine shall have completed their innings, and the other nine shall have equaled or exceeded the score of their opponents in their incompleted innings, in which case the game shall be decided by the total score obtained, which score shall be recorded as the score of the game.

Ending a Game. SEC. 9. When the umpire calls "Game," it shall end, but when he merely suspends play for any stated period, it may be resumed at the point at which it was suspended; provided such suspension does not extend beyond the day of the match.

RULE III.

SEC. 1.- Any player who shall, in any way, **Betting prohibited.** be interested in any bet or wager on any League game, or who shall purchase or have purchased for him any "pool" or chance, sold or given away, shall be expelled.

SEC. 2. Any player who shall conspire with any person whatever, against the interests of his club, or by any conduct manifest a disposition to obstruct the management of his club, may be expelled by his club.

SEC. 3. The club is entitled to the best services of the player, and if any player becomes indifferent or careless in his play, or from any cause becomes unable to render service satisfactory to his club, the club may, at its option, refuse to pay salary for such time or cancel the contract of said player.

RULE IV.—PITCHING.

SEC. 1. The pitcher's position shall be **The pitcher's position.** within a space of ground six feet square, the front line of which shall be distant forty-five feet from the center of the home base, and the center of the square shall be equidistant from the first and the third bases. Each corner of the square shall be marked by a flat iron plate or stone six inches square fixed in the ground even with the surface.

SEC. 2. The player who delivers the ball to **Delivering the ball** the bat must do so while wholly within the lines of pitcher's position. He must remain within them until the ball has left his hand, and he shall not make any motion to deliver the ball to the bat while any part of his person is outside the lines of the pitcher's position. The ball must be delivered to the bat with the arm swinging nearly perpendicular at the side of the body, and the hand in swinging forward must pass below the hip.

A Foul Delivery. SEC. 3. Should the pitcher deliver the ball by an overhand throw, a "foul balk" shall be declared. Any outward swing of the arm, or any other swing save that of the perpendicular movement referred to in Section 2 of this rule, shall be considered an overhand throw.

Foul Balk. SEC. 4. When a "foul balk" is called, the umpire shall warn the pitcher of the penalty incurred by such unfair delivery, and should such delivery be continued until *three foul balks* have been called in one inning, the umpire shall declare the game forfeited.

Balking. SEC. 5. Should the pitcher make any motion to deliver the ball to the bat and fail so to deliver it—except the ball be accidentally dropped —or should he unnecessarily delay the game by not delivering the ball to the bat, or should he, when in the act of delivering the ball, have any part of his person outside the lines of his position, the umpire shall call a "balk," and players occupying the bases shall take one base each.

Good balls. SEC. 6. Every ball fairly delivered and sent in to the bat over the home base and at the height called for by the batsman shall be considered a good ball.

Called balls. SEC. 7. All balls delivered to the bat which are not sent in over the home base and at the height called for by the batsman shall be considered unfair balls, and every third ball so delivered must be called. When "three balls" have been called, the striker shall take first base, and all players who are thereby forced to leave a base shall take one base. Neither a "ball" nor a "strike" shall be called until the ball has passed the home base.

SEC. 8. All balls delivered to the bat which *Dead balls.* shall touch the striker's bat without being struck at, or his (the batsman's) person while standing in his position, or which shall hit the person of the umpire—unless they be passed balls, shall be considered *dead* balls, and shall be so called by the umpire, and no players shall be put out, base be run, or run be scored on any such ball; but if a dead ball be also an unfair ball, it shall be counted as one of the nine unfair balls which shall entitle the striker to a base.

RULE V.—BATTING DEPARTMENT.

SECTION 1. The batsman's or striker's *The batsman's position.* position shall be within a space of ground located on either side of the home base, six feet long by three feet wide, extending three feet in front of and three feet behind the line of the home base, and with its nearest line distant one foot from the home base.

SEC. 2. The batsmen must take their po- *The order of striking.* sitions in the order in which they are named on the score-book. After the first inning, the first striker in each inning shall be the batsman whose name follows that of the third man out in the preceding inning.

SEC 3. Any batsman failing to take his po- *Failing to take position.* sition at the bat in his order of striking— unless by reason of illness or injury, or by consent of the captains of the contesting nines— shall be declared out, unless the error be discovered before a fair ball has been struck, or the striker put out.

SEC. 4. Any batsman failing to take his po- *Refusing to strike.* sition at the bat within *one minute* after the umpire has called for the striker shall be declared out.

Specifying balls. SEC. 5. The batsman, on taking his position, must call for either a "*high ball*," a "*low ball*," or a "*fair ball*," and the umpire shall notify the pitcher to deliver the ball as required; such call shall not be changed after the first ball delivered.

Good balls to the bat. SEC. 6. A "*high ball*" shall be one sent in above the belt of the batsman, but not higher than his shoulder. A "*low ball*" shall be one sent in at the height of the belt, or between that height and the knee, but not higher than his belt. A "*fair ball*" shall be one between the range of shoulder high and the knee of the striker. All the above must be over the home base, and when fairly delivered, shall be considered fair balls to the bat.

Calling strikes. SEC. 7. Should the batsman fail to strike at the ball he calls for, or should he strike at and fail to hit the ball, the umpire shall call "one strike," and "two strikes," should he again fail. When two strikes have been called, should the batsman not strike at the next "good ball," the umpire shall warn him by calling "fair ball." But should he strike at and fail to hit the ball, or should he fail to strike at or to hit the next good ball, "three strikes" must be called, and the batsman must run to first base as in the case of hitting a fair ball.

A fair strike. SEC. 8. The batsman, when in the act of striking at the ball, must stand wholly within the lines of his position.

A foul strike. SEC. 9. Should the batsman step outside the lines of his position when he strikes the ball, the umpire shall call "foul strike and out," and base-runners shall return to the bases they occupied when the ball was hit.

SEC. 10. The foul lines shall be unlimited in length, and shall run from the right and left hand corners of the home base through the center of first and third bases to the foul posts, which shall be located at the boundary of the field and within the range of home and first base, and home and third base. Said lines shall be marked and on the inside, from base to base, with chalk, or some other white substance, so as to be plainly seen by the umpire. *The foul lines.*

SEC. 11. If the ball from a fair stroke of the bat first touches the ground, the person of a player, or any other object, either in front of, or on the foul ball lines, it shall be considered fair. *A fair hit ball.*

If the ball from a fair stroke of the bat first touches the ground, the person of a player, or any other object, behind the foul ball lines, it shall be declared foul, and the ball so hit shall be called foul by the umpire even before touching the ground, if it be seen falling foul. *A foul hit ball.*

The following are exceptions to the foregoing section : All balls batted directly to the ground that bound or roll within the foul lines between home and first or home and third bases, without first touching the person of a player, shall be considered fair. All balls batted directly to the ground that bound or roll outside the foul lines between home and first or home and third bases, without first touching the person of a player, shall be considered foul. In either of these cases the first point of contact between the batted ball and the ground shall not be regarded.

SEC. 12. When the batsman has fairly struck a fair ball, he shall vacate his position, and he shall then be considered a base-runner until he is put out or scores his run. *When batsmen become base-runners.*

How batsmen are put out.

SEC. 13. The batsman shall be declared out by the umpire as follows :

On the fly.

If a fair or foul ball be caught before touching the ground, provided it be not caught in a player's hat or cap.

On the bound.

If a foul ball be similarly held, or after touching the ground but once.

At first base.

If a fair ball be securely held by a fielder while touching first base with any part of his person before the base runner touches said base.

On three strikes.

If after three strikes have been called, he fails to touch first base before the ball is legally held there.

If after three strikes have been called, the ball be caught before touching the ground or after touching the ground but once.

If he plainly attempts to hinder the catcher from catching the ball, evidently without effort to make a fair strike, or makes a "foul strike."

RULE VI.—RUNNING THE BASES.

Touching the bases.

SECTION 1. Players running bases must touch each base in regular order, viz: first, second, third and home bases ; and when obliged to return to bases they have occupied they must retouch them in reverse order, both when running on fair and foul balls. In the latter case the base-runner must return to the base where he belongs on the run and not at a walk. No base shall be considered as having been occupied or held until it has been touched.

Forced off a base

SEC. 2. No player running the bases shall be forced to vacate the base he occupies unless the batsman becomes a base-runner. Should the first base be occupied by a base-runner when a fair ball is struck, the base-runner shall cease to be entitled to hold said base until the player running to first base shall be put out. The same rule shall apply in the case of the occupancy of the other bases under similar circumstances. No base-runner shall be forced to vacate the base he occupies if the base-runner succeeding him is not thus obliged to vacate his base.

SEC. 3.   Players forced to vacate their bases *How put out when forced.* may be put out by any fielders in the same manner as when running to first base.

SEC. 4.   The player running to first base shall *Overrunning first base.* be at liberty to overrun said base without his being put out for being off the base after first touching it, provided that in so overrunning the base he make no attempt to run to second base. In such case he must return at once and retouch first base, and after retouching said base he can be put out as at any other base.   If in so overrunning first base, he also attempts to run to second base, he shall forfeit such exemption from being put out.

SEC. 5.   Any player running a base who *Running out of the line of bases.* shall run beyond three feet from the line from base to base in order to avoid being touched by the ball in the hands of a fielder shall be declared out by the umpire, with or without appeal, but in case a fielder be occupying the runner's proper path attempting to field a batted ball, then the runner shall run out of the path and behind said fielder, and shall not be declared out for so doing.

SEC. 6.   One run shall be scored every time *When a run is scored.* a base-runner, after having regularly touched the first three bases, shall touch the home base before three hands are out.   If the third hand out is forced out, or is put out before reaching first base, a run shall not be scored.

SEC. 7.   When a "balk" is called by the *Taking bases on balks.* umpire, every player running the bases shall take one base without being put out, and shall do so on the run.

Taking bases on called balls. SEC. 8. When three "balls" have been called by the umpire, the batsman shall take one base, provided he do so on the run, without being put out, and should any base-runner be forced thereby to vacate his base, he also shall take one base. Each base-runner thus given a base shall be at liberty to run to other bases besides the base given, but only at the risk of being put out in so running.

Holding a base. SEC. 9. A base-runner shall be considered as holding a base, viz., entitled to occupy it, until he shall have regularly touched the next base in order.

Running bases on fair and foul fly balls. SEC. 10. No base shall be run or run be scored when a fair or foul ball has been caught or momentarily held before touching the ground, unless the base held when the ball was hit is retouched by the base-runner after the ball has been so caught or held by the fielder.

Returning to bases on foul ground balls. SEC. 11. No run or base can be made upon a foul ball that shall touch the ground before being caught or held by a fielder, and any player running bases shall return, without being put out, to the base he occupied when the ball was struck, and remain on such base until the ball is held by the pitcher.

SEC. 12. Any player running the bases on fair or foul balls caught before touching the ground must return to the base he occupied when the ball was struck, and retouch such base before attempting to make another or score a run, and said player shall be liable to be put out in so returning, as in the case of running to first base when a fair ball is hit and not caught flying.

SEC. 13. If the player running the bases is *Obstructing base-runners.* prevented from making a base by the obstruction of an adversary, he shall be entitled to that base and shall not be put out.

SEC. 14. No player shall be allowed a substitute in running the bases, except for illness *Substitutes in running bases.* or injury; in such a case the opposing captain shall select the man to run as substitute.

SEC. 15. Any player running the bases shall be declared out if, at any time, while the ball *How base-runners are put out.* is in play, he be touched by the ball in the hand of a fielder, without some part of his person is touching a base.

If a ball be held by a fielder on the first base *Preference given to the base-runner.* before the base-runner, after hitting a fair ball, touches that base, he shall be declared out.

Any base-runner failing to touch the base he *Failing to touch a base.* runs for shall be declared out if the ball be held by a fielder, while touching said base, before the base-runner returns and touches it.

Any base-runner who shall in any way inter- *Obstructing a fielder.* fere with or obstruct a fielder while attempting to catch a fair fly ball, or a foul ball, shall be declared out. If he willfully obstructs a fielder from fielding a ball, he shall be declared out, and, if a batted ball strike him, he shall be declared out.

If a base-runner, in running from home to first base, shall run inside the foul line, or more than three feet outside of it, he shall be declared out.

RULE VII.—THE UMPIRE AND HIS DUTIES.

SECTION 1. Before the beginning of the *Selecting an umpire.* playing season, the League shall select three gentlemen of good repute, competent to act as umpires, and who are residents in each city (or

immediate locality) where there is a League club.
At least three hours before each championship
game, the manager of the visiting club shall, in
the presence of the manager of the home club,
draw one of the three names of gentlemen so
designated for that city, who shall immediately
be notified by the manager of the home club to
act as umpire for the game in question. In
case of inability of either or all of such three
gentleman to act as umpire, the captains of the
contesting nines shall, by lot, choose an umpire.

Changing an umpire.
SEC. 2. The umpire shall not be changed
during the progress of a match game, except
for reason of illness or injury, or by the consent
of the captains of the two contesting nines, in
case he shall have willfully violated the rules of
the game.

Special duties.
SEC. 3. Before the commencement of a
match, the umpire shall see that the rules
governing the materials of the game, and also
those applicable to the positions of batsmen and
pitcher, are strictly observed. Also that the
fence in the rear of the catcher's position is
distant not less than ninety feet from the home
base, except it mark the boundary line of the
field, in which case the umpire, for every ball
passing the catcher and touching the fence,
shall give each base-runner one base without
his being put out.

Special ground rules.
Before calling "play," the umpire shall ask
the captain of the home club whether there are
any special ground rules to be enforced, and if
there are, he shall see that they are duly enforced, provided they do not conflict with any
rules of the game.

Reversing decisions.
SEC. 4. No decision rendered by the umpire
on any point of play in base-running shall be

reversed upon the testimony of any of the players. But if it shall be shown by the captain of either of the contesting clubs that the umpire has palpably misinterpreted the rules, or given an erroneous decision, he shall reverse said decision.

SEC. 5. Should the umpire be unable to see whether a catch has been fairly made or not, he shall be at liberty to appeal to the bystanders, and to render his decision according to the fairest testimony at command. *Decisions on catches.*

SEC. 6. No person, not engaged in the game, shall be permitted to occupy any position within the lines of the field of contest, or in any way interrupt the umpire during the progress of the game. No player except the captain or player especially designated by him shall address the umpire concerning any point of play in dispute, and any violation of this rule shall subject the offender to an immediate reprimand by the umpire. *Interfering with the umpire.*

SEC. 7. The umpire shall require the players on the batting side who are not at the bat or running the bases, to keep at a distance of not less than fifty feet from the line of home and first base and home and third base, or further off if he so decide. The captain and one assistant only shall be permitted to coach players running the bases, and they must not approach within fifteen feet of the foul lines. *Interfering with players.*

SEC. 8. Should any fielder stop or catch the ball with his hat, cap, or any part of his dress, the umpire should call "dead ball," and the base-runners shall each be entitled to two bases for any fair hit ball so stopped or caught. Should the ball be stopped by any person not engaged in the game, the umpire must call "dead ball," and players running bases at the *Unfair fielding and dead balls.*

time shall be entitled to the bases they were running for, and the ball be regarded as dead until settled in the hands of the pitcher while standing within the lines of his position.

Violation of rules.   SEC. 9.   Any match game in which the umpire shall declare any section of this code of rules to have been willfully violated shall at once be declared by him to have been forfeited by the club at fault.

SEC. 10.   No manager, captain or player shall address the audience, except in case of necessary explanation; and any manager, captain, or player, who shall use abusive, threatening or improper language to the audience, shall be punished by suspension from play for twenty days and forfeiture of his salary for such period.

SEC. 11. No section of these Rules shall be construed as conflicting with or affecting any article of the Constitution.

RULE VIII.—SCORING.

In order to promote uniformity in scoring championship games, the following instructions, suggestions and definitions are made for the benefit of scorers of League clubs, and they are required to make the scores mentioned in Sec. 9, Art. XIII, of the League Constitution in accordance therewith.

BATTING.

SECTION 1.   The first item in the tabulated score, after the player's name and position, shall be the number of times he has been at bat during the game.   Any time or times where the player has been sent to base on called balls shall not be included in this column.

SEC. 2.   In the second column should be set down the runs made by each player.

MEETING

of the

DIRECTORS OF THE NATIONAL LEAGUE

of

PROFESSIONAL BASE BALL CLUBS,

HELD AT THE

Kennard House, Cleveland, Ohio, Thursday, Dec. 7th, A. D. 1876.

———————•———————

Present—Messrs. CHASE, FOWLE, FERGUSON and APOLLONIO.

The President being absent, Mr. CHASE was chosen President *pro tem.* On the motion of Mr. FOWLE, the Board proceeded to business.

The Secretary submitted a tabular statement of games won and lost by each of the contesting League Clubs during the season of 1876, showing the *Chicago Club* to have won the championship. Mr. FOWLE moved that the games remaining unplayed by the *Athletic* and *Mutual* clubs be declared forfeited by a score of nine runs to none, and that the Secretary's report be so amended as to include the same. Lost. The Secretary's report was then adopted, Mr. FOWLE voting in the negative. Mr. J. A. DEVLIN presented an appeal in writing, asking his release from the *Louisville Club*, claiming that the club had failed to comply with the conditions of his contract. Mr. CHASE presented a counter statement. On motion of Mr. APOLLONIO, Mr. DEVLIN was granted leave to withdraw his appeal. Mr. FERGUSON presented written charges against Mr. BOND, and asked his expulsion. The Chair ruled that the charges could not be entertained. A communication was received from the four Western clubs, recommending that the *Athletic* and *Mutual* clubs be declared as having forfeited their membership in the League on account of their failure to play games due to the said clubs. Mr. THOMPSON, having been sent for, acknowledged the facts, as stated, to be true, and requested that he be heard before the League.

On motion of Mr. FOWLE, the following resolution was adopted:

" *Resolved*, That the *Athletic Base Ball Club,* of Philadelphia, Pa., and the *Mutual Base Ball Club,* of Brooklyn, N. Y., have forfeited their membership in this League."

Mr. APOLLONIO moved that the request of Mr. THOMPSON, in being heard before the League, be granted. Carried. A communication was received from Messrs. ANSON, BATTIN and BRADLEY, asking their release from engagements with the *Athletic Base Ball Club* for reasons stated. The Board decided that they had no jurisdiction, and directed the Secretary to present the same to the League.

The report of the Secretary and Treasurer was presented, and, on motion, it was accepted and ordered placed on file. On motion, the Board adjourned to meet on the following day, at ten o'clock A. M., or at the call of the Chairman.

TURSDAY, Dec. 7. A. D. 1876.

Board met at 11 o'clock A. M. *Present*—Messrs. CHASE, FOWLE, APOLLONIO and FERGUSON. On motion of Mr. FOWLE, the action of the Board in relation to the communication of Messrs. ANSON, BATTIN and BRADLEY was reconsidered. Without further action, the communication was again referred to the League. No further business appearing, on motion adjourned.

Signed,   CHAS. E. CHASE,
               ROBT. FERGUSON,
               CHAS. A. FOWLE,
               N. T. APOLLONIO,
                          Directors.

ANNUAL MEETING

OF THE

NATIONAL LEAGUE

OF

PROFESSIONAL BASE BALL CLUBS;

HELD AT THE

Kennard House, Cleveland, Ohio, Thursday, Dec. 7th, A. D. 1876.

12:30 P. M. The meeting was called to order by Mr. C. E. Chase, President pro tem. The following gentlemen presented their credentials:

N. T. Apollonio. and Harry Wright, representing the Boston B. B. C.; C. E. Chase and C. W. Johnstone, representing the Louisville B. B. C.; W. A. Hulbert, and A. G. Mills, representing the Chicago B. B. C.; Robert Ferguson, representing the Hartford B. B. C.; Chas. A. Fowle, representing the St. Louis B. B. C.; J. L. Keck, representing the Cincinnati B. B. C.; George W. Thompson, representing the Athletic B. B. C.

The President being absent, Mr. Apollonio was chosen President pro tem. Mr. Hulbert moved that the following be the order of business. Carried.

1st. Reading minutes of last meeting.

2d. Report of Secretary.

3d. Report of Board of Directors.

4th. Miscellaneous business.

5th. Amendments of constitution.

6th. Amendments of playing rules.

7th. Election of new members.

8th. Election of officers.

9th. Adjournment.

On motion, the reading of the minutes of the last meeting was dispensed with. The Board of Directors submitted their report. On motion of Mr. Mills, the report was received. Mr. Keck moved that Mr. Thompson be heard in defense of his club. Mr. Thompson submitted a written statement in defense. Mr. Mills called for the reading of the communication from the four Western clubs, and moved the adoption of the resolution therein recommended. Carried. Mr. Wright moved that when the vote upon expulsion is taken, it be by yeas and nays. Carried. Mr. Keck offered the following:

Whereas, the League having adopted the resolution of the Board of Directors of 1876, as follows: *Resolved*, that the Athletic Base Ball Club of Philadelphia, Pa., and the Mutual Base Ball Club of Brooklyn, N. Y., have forfeited their membership in this League; therefore.

Be it resolved, that, in accordance with the adoption of said resolution, the Athletic Base Ball Club of Philadelphia, Pa., and the Mutual Base Ball Club of Brooklyn, N. Y., be, and the same are hereby, expelled from this League. Upon the roll being called, the vote of every club was recorded in the affirmative.

The communication of Messrs. Anson, Battin and Bradley was read, and, on motion, it was laid on the table.

Mr. Ferguson called for the reading of charges preferred by him against Mr. Bond. The Chair ruled that the communication could not be received. Mr. Keck appealed from the decision of the Chair. The Chair was sustained. The meeting next proceeded to consider proposed amendments to the Constitution, which, as amended, were adopted as follows: (See Constitution.)

On motion, a proposition made by Mr. L. H. Mahn, of Boston, Mass., to furnish a uniform ball for the use of the League, was accepted, the object being to secure a uniform ball as per sample selected. On motion, it was ordered that the Secretary shall inspect and stamp all balls to be furnished to the League Clubs.

Pending the consideration of amendments to the playing rules, the meeting adjourned to meet on the following day at 9:30 A. M.

FRIDAY, Dec. 8, A. D. 1876.

Meeting called to order at 10.20 A. M., and resumed the consideration of amendments to the playing rules, which, as amended, were adopted as follows: (See Rules.)

The following resolution was adopted:

Resolved, That on and after March 15, 1877, no League Club shall employ or play in its nine any player to whose services any other club of good standing, either in or out of the League, is entitled by legal contract."

On motion, It was *Resolved*, that the publication of the "Official Book" be left in the hands of the Secretary.

Mr. Ferguson moved that when we adjourn, it be to meet at the Kennard House, Cleveland, Ohio, at the time called for in the Constitution. Carried.

On motion, a vote of thanks was tendered to the proprietor of the Kennard House, for kind and courteous treatment received, and facilities extended the League during its session.

Mr. Keck offered the following resolution:

"*Resolved*, That Messrs. Hulbert and Wright be appointed a committee on schedule, and they are hereby authorized as follows: Mr. Hulbert to submit the Western schedule, and Mr. Wright the Eastern. Both shall arrange and submit a schedule for games between the East and West. They shall submit the same to all clubs directly interested, who shall endorse their approval or disapproval and forward the same to the Secretary of the League. If a majority agree, the Secretary to notify each club of said agreement. If the majority should disagree, the committee shall submit an amended schedule to be agreed to as before."

Mr. Fowle offered the following resolution, which was adopted :

Resolved, That the League desires to express to to Mr. Young, Secretary of the League, its high appreciation of the faithful and efficient manner in which he has discharged the duties of his office during the initial year of the League.

In the selection of Umpires, it was agreed that each club shall, prior to March 1st, of each year, send to the Secretary the names of not less than five persons of good repute and who are competent to act, and resident of the city or immediate vicinity where the club is located. The lists of persons so submitted shall be, by the Secretary, transmitted to every club—except the club proposing same—and the three persons on each list receiving the greatest number of approvals shall be the persons selected to act under the provisions of Sec. 1, Rule VII, of Playing Rules in their respective districts.

The meeting next proceeded to select a Board of Directors, with the following result:

—— ——, Boston B. B. Club.
C. E. Chase, Louisville B. B. Club.
M. G. Bulkeley, Hartford B. B. Club.
W. A. Hulbert, Chicago B. B. Club.
Charles A. Fowle, St. Louis B. B. Club.

Mr. Hulbert nominated Mr. Apollonio for President of the League, but Mr. A. declined the honor, whereupon Mr. W. A. Hulbert was unanimously elected.

On motion of Mr. Chase, Mr. N. E. Young was reelected Secretary, and his salary fixed at five hundred dollars ($500) per annum.

No further business appearing, on motion, adjourned to meet at the Kennard House, Cleveland, Ohio, on Wednesday, December 5, A. D. 1877, at 12 o'clock noon, unless sooner convened by order of the President.

(Signed) W. A. HULBERT,
N. E. Young, *President.*
Secretary.

48

SPECIAL CLUB RULES FOR 1877.

The parties hereto agree that, during the ball playing season of 1877, in consideration of the advantages to each of a uniform system of club rules, and of division of gate receipts, each club subscribing hereto, shall pay to every other club subscribing hereto, for each championship game of ball in which such other club shall, as "visiting club," contest against it upon its own grounds, the sum of fifteen (15) cents for each and every person admitted to such grounds to witness such game, or any part thereof, or admitted to such grounds for any other purpose, prior to such game, and remaining after its commencement, excepting only players of the contesting clubs, policemen in uniform, and ten (10) other persons. We further agree that for the purposes of this agreement, a "game" shall be that in which one full inning shall be played by the contesting clubs, in accordance with the playing rules of the League. The number of persons admitted to the grounds shall be determined by the use of the necessary number of self-registering turnstiles, the keys of which shall be delivered to the agent of the visiting club before the opening of the grounds for each game, and such agent of the visiting club shall also have the right to affix a seal to the register or box of such turnstile. We further agree that we will pay for the services of the umpire a sum not exceeding five dollars ($5) per game; the home club to pay same, and if extra expense be incurred in securing the attendance of such umpire, the contesting clubs shall equally divide said extra expense.

We further agree, and do hereby notify all players now under contract, or that may hereafter contract with either club subscribing hereto, that each player must pay thirty dollars ($30) for the uniform furnished him by the club for the season of 1877, and must, at his own expense, keep the same clean and in good repair, and that, while absent with his club upon a tour or tours, during the season of 1877, the sum of fifty cents per day will be deducted from his pay. And we further agree that we will not engage or play any player that may be released by any club subscribing hereto, on account of disagreement between such player and his club, growing out of any stipulation of this agreement.

In witness whereof, the parties hereto have hereunto set their names, in the City of Cleveland, State of Ohio, this eighth day of December, A. D. 1876.

> THE CHICAGO BALL CLUB,
>> *By W. A. Hulbert, Pres't.*
>
> THE CINCINNATI BALL CLUB,
>> *By J. L. Keck & Bros.*
>
> THE LOUISVILLE BASE BALL CLUB,
>> *By Chas. E. Chase, Vice Pres't.*
>
> THE BOSTON BASE BALL ASSOCIATION,
>> *By N. T. Appolonio, Pres't.*
>
> THE HARTFORD BASE BALL CLUB,
>> *By Robert Ferguson.*
>
> THE ST. LOUIS BASE BALL CLUB,
>> *By Chas. A. Fowle, Secretary.*

BATTING AVERAGES

Of Players who have taken part in six or more Championship Games.

Rank.	NAME.	CLUB.	Number of games played.	Times at bat.	Runs.	1st Bases.	Percentage of base hits per time at bat.	Average runs per game.
1	Barnes	Chicago	66	342	126	138	.403	1.90
2	Hall	Athletic	60	276	51	98	.355	0.85
3	Peters	Chicago	66	319	70	111	.348	1.06
4	McVey	Chicago	63	310	62	107	.345	0.98
5	Anson	Chicago	66	321	63	110	.342	0·95
6	Clinton	Louisville	16	65	8	22	.338	0.50
7	Myerle	Athletic	55	259	46	87	.336	0.84
8	White	Chicago	66	310	66	104	.335	1.00
9	Hines	Chicago	64	308	62	101	.330	0.97
10	Higham	Hartford	67	314	59	102	.325	0.88
11	Pike	St. Louis	63	290	55	91	.314	0.87
12	O'Rourke,	Boston	70	327	61	102	.312	0.87
	Devlin,	Louisville	68	301	38	94	.312	0.56
13	Spalding,	Chicago	66	298	54	91	.305	0.85
	Andrus,	Chicago	8	36	6	11	.305	0.75
14	Carey	Hartford	68	292	51	78	.301	0.76
15	Clapp	St. Louis	64	308	60	91	.297	0.94
16	Eggler	Athletic	39	176	28	52	.295	0.72
17	Battin	St. Louis	64	289	34	85	.294	0.53
18	Sutton	Athletic	54	239	45	70	.292	0.83
19	Wright,	Boston	70	343	72	100	.291	1.03
	Glenn,	Chicago	66	288	55	84	.291	0.83
20	Fisler	Athletic	59	280	42	80	.286	0.71
21	Jones	Cincinnati	64	283	40	79	.279	0.62
22	Hallinan,	Mutual	54	242	45	67	.277	0.83
	Leonard,	Boston	64	307	53	85	.277	0.83
	Remsen,	Hartford	69	325	62	89	.277	0.90
23	Murnan	Boston	69	316	60	87	.275	0.87
	Sturt,	Mutual	56	205	40	73	.275	0.71
24	Bond	Hartford	45	182	18	50	.274	0.40
25	Addy,	Chicago	33	147	36	40	.272	1.09
	Fulmer,	Louisville	66	268	28	73	.272	0.42
26	Cassidy	Hartford	12	48	6	13	.271	0.50
27	Holdsworth,	Mutual	52	242	23	64	.264	0.44
	Ferguson,	Hartford	69	314	48	83	.264	0.69
28	Hague	Louisville	67	296	31	78	.263	0.40
29	McGeary,	St. Louis	60	278	48	72	.259	0.80
	Morrill,	Boston	66	281	38	73	.259	0.58
	Mills,	Hartford	63	255	23	66	.259	0.44
	Manning,	Boston	70	295	52	76	.257	0.74
30	Dean,	Cincinnati	34	140	9	36	.257	0.26
	Gerhardt,	Louisville	65	295	33	76	.257	0.51

Batting Averages—*Continued.*

Rank.	NAME.	CLUB.	Number of games played.	Times at bat.	Runs.	1st Bases.	Percentage of base hits per time at bat.	Average runs per game.
31	Allison, }	Hartford	43	164	19	42	.256	0.44
	Holbert, }	Louisville	12	43	3	11	.256	0.25
32	Booth, }	Cincinnati	63	281	31	71	.253	0.49
33	Hastings, }	Louisville	67	288	36	73	.253	0.54
34	Kessler	Cincinnati	59	255	26	64	.251	0.44
	Ritterson	Athletic	15	52	8	13	.250	0.53
35	Burdock, }	Hartford	69	322	66	80	.249	0.95
	York, }	Hartford	67	273	47	68	.249	0.70
36	Knight, }	Athletic	55	242	32	60	.248	0.58
	Schafer, }	Boston	70	290	47	72	.248	0.67
37	Fisher, }	Cincinnati	35	129	12	32	.248	0.34
	Ryan	Louisville	65	247	32	61	.247	0.49
38	Bradley, }	St. Louis	64	268	29	66	.246	0.45
	Gould, }	Cincinnati	61	264	27	65	.246	0.44
39	Cuthbert	St. Louis	62	289	46	70	.242	0.74
40	Whitney, }	Boston	34	140	27	33	.235	0.80
	Chapman, }	Louisville	17	68	4	16	.235	0.23
41	Pierson, }	Cincinnati	56	234	33	55	.235	0.59
42	Blong	St. Louis	62	260	30	62	.233	0.53
43	Hicks	Mutual	45	191	20	44	.230	0.44
44	Malone	Athletic	22	96	14	22	.229	0.64
	Force	Athletic	80	289	48	66	.228	0.80
45	Bradley, }	Boston	22	84	12	19	.228	0.54
	Foley, }	Cincinnati	58	221	19	50	.228	0.33
46	Coons	Athletic	54	222	30	50	.225	0.56
47	Craver	Mutual	56	248	24	55	.222	0.43
48	Booth	Mutual	57	230	17	49	.212	0.30
49	Zettlein, }	Athletic	32	128	11	27	.211	0.31
	Harbidge }	Hartford	30	109	11	23	.211	0.37
50	Treacy,	Mutual	57	257	47	54	.210	0.82
51	Brown	Boston	45	193	23	41	.207	0.51
52	Bielaski	Chicago	31	141	24	29	.205	0.77
53	Mack, }	St. Louis	48	191	32	39	.204	0.67
	Allison, }	Louisville	31	132	9	27	.204	0.29
54	Sweasy	Cincinnati	56	227	18	46	.202	0.32
55	"Josephs"	Boston	32	124	19	25	.201	0.78
56	Pearce, }	St. Louis	25	105	12	21	.200	0.48
	Williams, }	Cincinnati	9	35	1	7	.200	0.11
57	Snyder	Louisville	56	226	21	44	.194	0.37
58	Somerville	Louisville	64	257	20	48	.187	0.45
59	Bechtel	Louisville	14	55	2	10	.182	0.14
60	Mathews	Mutual	56	221	19	40	.181	0.34
61	Dehlman, }	St. Louis	64	254	40	45	.177	0.62
	Nichols, }	Mutual	57	214	20	38	.177	0.35
62	Cummings	Hartford	24	105	14	17	.162	0.58
63	Carbine	Louisville	6	25	3	4	.140	0.50
64	Clack	Cincinnati	31	123	10	19	.154	0.32
65	McGinley, }	Boston	9	40	5	6	.150	0.66
	Snyder, }	Cincinnati	56	200	10	31	.150	0.18
66	Youser	Athletic	21	59	11	12	.135	0.52

FIELDING AVERAGES

Of Players who have taken part in six or more
Championship Games.

FIRST BASEMEN.

Rank.	NAME.	CLUB.	Number of games played.	Number put out.	Times assisting.	Fielding errors.	Total number of chances.	Percentage of chances accepted.
1	Fisler	Athletic	13	131	3	3	137	.978
2	Start	Mutual	56	647	10	21	578	.963
	Glenn	Chicago	10	103	0	4	107	.962
8	Dehlman	St. Louis	64	750	8	33	791	.958
	Allison	Louisville	8	90	1	4	95	.958
4	McVey	Chicago	55	495	10	23	528	.936
5	Gerhardt	Louisville	53	657	13	40	710	.944
6	Mills	Hartford	63	644	7	42	693	.939
	Knight	Athletic	10	89	3	6	98	.939
7	Gould	Cincinnati	61	584	13	39	636	.938
8	Murnan	Boston	65	689	5	55	749	.929
9	Zettlein	Athletic	6	57	2	5	64	.922
10	Sutton	Athletic	30	324	11	31	366	.915
11	Carbine	Louisville	6	71	1	10	82	.878

SECOND BASEMEN.

1	Gerhardt	Louisville	6	20	18	2	40	.950
2	Barnes	Chicago	66	167	199	36	402	.910
8	Burdock	Hartford	69	211	175	45	431	.895
4	McGeary	St. Louis	55	132	180	39	351	.889
5	Somerville	Louisville	61	210	251	69	530	.869
6	Sweasy	Cincinnati	55	167	159	51	376	.864
7	Clack	Cincinnati	8	21	22	7	50	.860
8	Morrill	Boston	37	105	117	37	259	.857
9	Leonard	Boston	29	89	81	29	199	.854
10	Fisler	Athletic	21	45	66	22	133	.834
11	Sutton	Athletic	15	47	32	16	95	.831
12	Fouser	Athletic	14	37	60	20	107	.813
	Craver	Mutual	41	95	84	41	220	.813

FIELDING AVERAGES—*Continued.*

THIRD BASEMEN.

Rank.	NAME.	CLUB.	Number of games played.	Number put out.	Times assisting.	Fielding errors.	Total number of chances.	Percentage of chances accepted.
1	Battin	St. Louis	63	115	145	40	300	.867
2	Anson	Chicago	66	137	147	50	334	.850
3	Ferguson	Hartford	69	124	133	54	311	.826
4	Schafer	Boston	70	122	146	63	331	.809
5	Myerle	Athletic	48	84	101	49	214	.700
6	Nichols }	Mutual	57	123	135	73	331	.779
7	Foley }	Cincinnati	46	89	96	52	236	.779
8	Booth	Cincinnati	20	32	27	18	77	.766
9	Hague	Louisville	67	67	90	52	209	.751
	Sutton	Athletic	7	11	8	8	27	.704

SHORT STOPS.

Rank.	NAME.	CLUB.	Number of games played.	Number put out.	Times assisting.	Fielding errors.	Total number of chances.	Percentage of chances accepted.
1	Peters	Chicago	66	95	193	21	309	.932
2	Pearce	St. Louis	23	23	87	12	122	.901
3	Force	Athletic	59	108	237	39	384	.898
4	Wright }	Boston	66	89	251	43	383	.886
5	Black }	St. Louis	41	42	114	20	176	.886
6	Carey	Hartford	68	74	218	39	331	.882
7	Fulmer	Louisville	66	83	209	47	339	.861
8	Booth	Cincinnati	20	33	54	18	105	.828
9	Kessler	Cincinnati	44	56	115	45	216	.791
	Hallinan	Mutual	50	45	172	67	284	.764

CATCHERS.

Rank.	NAME.	CLUB.	Number of games played.	Number put out.	Times assisting.	Fielding errors.	Total number of chances.	Percentage of chances accepted.
1	Allison	Hartford	38	201	43	45	289	.844
2	White	Chicago	64	303	50	93	446	.791
3	Holbert	Louisville	12	62	24	23	100	.780
4	Snyder	Louisville	53	249	86	92	427	.784
5	Clapp	St. Louis	61	333	56	108	497	.783
6	Brown	Boston	44	187	45	75	307	.765
7	Hartidge	Hartford	20	93	29	40	162	.753
8	Morrill	Boston	23	94	43	55	188	.707
9	Craver	Mutual	11	57	21	34	112	.696
10	Hicks	Mutual	45	222	47	122	391	.688
11	Foley	Cincinnati	12	51	13	30	94	.681
12	Higham	Hartford	11	38	8	24	70	.657
13	Malone	Athletic	19	77	30	56	163	.656
14	Pierson	Cincinnati	26	112	43	85	240	.646
15	Booth	Cincinnati	22	74	31	64	169	.621
16	Coons	Athletic	17	51	9	48	108	.555
17	Ritterson	Athletic	12	44	7	44	95	.537

FIELDING AVERAGES—*Continued.*

FIELDERS.

Rank	NAME.	CLUB.	Number of games played.	Number put out.	Times assisting.	Fielding errors.	Total number of chances.	Percentage of chances accepted.
1	Cassidy..	Hartford............	8	7	2	0	9	100.
2	Fisler....................	Athletic............	25	54	6	5	65	.923
3	Hines..................	Chicago............	64	159	8	15	182	.917
4	Leonard..............	Boston.............	35	68	6	7	81	.913
5	Eggler.................	Athletic............	39	109	6	11	126	.912
6	Collins................	Louisville........ ..	7	8	2	1	11	.909
7	Holdsworth.........	Mutual............	49	109	10	13	132	.901
8	York..................	Hartford	67	153	8	18	179	.899
9	Blong	St. Louis..........	62	64	15	9	88	.898
10	Pike..................	St. Louis..........	61	82	13	11	106	.896
11	Remsen...	Hartford..........	69	177	12	24	213	.887
12	Ryan................	Louisville.........	64	131	1	17	149	.886
13	Higham.............	Hartford..........	54	57	22	11	90	.877
14	Hastings............	Louisville	63	98	11	16	125	.872
15	Glenn	Chicago............	56	137	5	22	164	.866
16	Pierson.............	Cincinnati........	30	48	10	9	67	.865
17	Jones...............	Cincinnati........	64	151	11	27	189	.857
18	O'Rourke............	Boston............	68	154	7	27	188	.856
19	Treacy...............	Mutual......	57	202	9	39	250	.844
20	Cuthbert......	St. Louis..........	62	95	7	19	121	.843
21	Bechtel.............	Louisville..........	14	14	1	3	18	.833
22	Snyder.............	Cincinnati........	55	168	6	37	211	.824
23	Fisher..............	Cincinnati........	9	12	2	3	17	.823
24	Kessler.............	Cincinnati........	15	21	10	7	38	.816
25	Whitney............	Boston............	34	75	8	20	103	.806
26	Fouser.............	Athletic............	7	13	4	4	21	.809
27	Hall.................	Athletic............	60	156	7	30	196	.801
28	Addy................	Chicago...	33	46	6	13	65	.800
29	Allison	Louisville..........	23	34	11	12	57	.789
30	Harbidge............	Hartford..........	6	9	2	3	14	.786
31	Clinton.............	Louisville..........	14	14	4	5	23	.783
32	Manning............	Boston............	47	70	13	25	108	.768
33	Booth..............	Mutual............	53	73	11	26	110	.763
34	Bielaski.............	Chicago............	31	41	4	14	59	.762
35	Clack............'.....	Cincinnati..........	16	34	1	12	47	.745
36	Chapman............	Louisville..........	17	17	2	7	26	.731
37	Spalding .... }	Chicago............	6	6	4	4	14	.714
38	Andrus..... .... }	Chicago............	8	5	0	2	7	.714
39	Coons..............	Athletic............	29	40	7	20	67	.701
40	Knight..............	Athletic............	9	16	0	7	23	.696
41	"Josephs"...............	Boston.............	6	5	3	10	18	.444

PITCHERS' RECORD, IN ALPHABETICAL ORDER.

NAME.	CLUB.	Number of games played.	Times at bat of opponents.	Runs scored by opponents.	Average per game.	Percentage of runs scored per times at bat.	Runs earned by opponents.	Average per game.	Percentage of runs earned per times at bat.	Number of 1st bases made by opponents.	Average per game.	Percentage of base hits to times at bat of oppon'ts	Number put out.	Times assisted.	Fielding errors.	Total number of chances.	Percentage of chances accepted
Bond	Hartford	45	1609	164	3.64	.102	65	1.44	.040	351	7.93	.222	20	141	30	292	.821
Bradley	St. Louis	64	2283	229	3.58	.100	72	1.12	.036	480	7.50	.210	50	149	84	283	.703
Bradley	Boston	20	777	116	5.80	.149	43	2.15	.055	197	9.85	.253	12	29	18	59	.695
Cummings	Hartford	24	896	97	4.01	.108	40	1.66	.044	217	9.04	.242	9	53	24	86	.721
Dean	Cincinnati	30	1299	279	9.30	.215	103	3.43	.079	430	14.33	.331	22	57	54	133	.594
Devlin	Louisville	67	2580	329	4.91	.127	109	1.62	.042	587	8.76	.227	44	217	47	308	.847
Fisher	Cincinnati	25	1013	202	8.08	.199	72	2.88	.071	283	11.32	.279	22	45	24	91	.736
"Josephs"	Boston	23	947	158	6.87	.167	58	2.52	.061	257	11.17	.271	15	64	73	152	.585
Knight	Athletic	32	1368	288	9.00	.210	83	2.59	.061	391	12.22	.286	33	41	75	149	.497
Manning	Boston	18	718	96	5.33	.133	26	1.44	.036	167	9.28	.232	9	54	32	95	.663
Mathews	Mutual	56	2362	405	7.23	.171	138	2.46	.062	673	12.02	.285	41	83	51	175	.708
Spalding	Chicago	60	2248	236	3.93	.105	104	1.73	.046	567	9.45	.252	52	118	30	200	.850
Williams	Cincinnati	9	367	75	8.33	.204	36	4.00	.099	120	13.33	.327	10	17	9	36	.750
Zettlein	Athletic	25	1037	220	8.80	.202	85	3.40	.078	361	14.44	.332	10	41	15	66	.773

BATTING AND FIELDING RECORD

Of Clubs Members of the National League of Professional Base Ball Clubs,

SEASON OF 1876.

NAME OF CLUB	WHERE LOCATED	No. of Games played	No. of Games won	Times at bat	Runs scored	Average per game	Runs earned	Average per Errno.	1st Bases	Percentage of base hits per time at bat	Number put out	Times assisted	Fielding errors	Total chances	Percentage of chances accepted
Chicago	Chicago, Ill	66	52	2,818	624	9.45	267	4.03	926	.328	1,777	759	339	2,875	.882
Hartford	Hartford, Conn	69	47	2,703	429	6.22	154	2.23	711	.264	1,874	856	409	3,139	.869
St. Louis	St. Louis, Mo	64	45	2,536	386	6.03	109	1.70	642	.253	1,734	798	395	2,927	.865
Boston	Boston, Mass	70	39	2,780	471	6.73	167	2.38	723	.260	1,895	912	630	3,437	.818
Louisville	Louisville, Ky	69	30	2,504	280	4.06	107	1.55	641	.247	1,929	968	492	3,389	.854
Mutual	Brooklyn, N. Y	57	21	2,202	260	4.55	72	1.26	404	.223	1,593	634	541	2,768	.845
Athletic	Philadelphia, Pa	60	14	2,414	378	6.30	145	2.41	646	.267	1,653	728	656	3,037	.784
Cincinnati	Cincinnati, O	65	9	2,413	238	3.66	77	1.18	555	.230	1,772	741	616	3,129	.803
Total		520	257	20.460	3066	6.89	1098	2.11	5338	.261	14,227	6.336	4078	24,701	.835

Tie Games Played—LOUISVILLE, 3; ATHLETIC, 1; HARTFORD, 1; MUTUAL, 1.

RECORD OF CHAMPIONSHIP GAMES PLAYED
DURING THE SEASON OF 1876.

Number of Games.	Date.	Names of Contestants.	Where Played.	Winning Club.	Runs Scored. Win'g Club.	Runs Scored. Los'g Club.
1	April 22	Athletic vs. Boston...	Philadelphia, Pa.	Boston.........	6	5
2	" 24	Athletic vs. Boston...	Philadelphia, Pa.	Athletic......	20	3
3	" 25	Mutual vs. Boston.....	Brooklyn, N. Y...	Boston.........	7	6
4	" 25	Chicago vs. Louisville	Louisville, Ky....	Chicago.......	4	0
5	" 25	Cincin'ti vs. St. Louis	Cincinnati, O......	Cincinnati...	2	1
6	" 27	Hartford vs. Mutual..	Brooklyn, N. Y...	Mutual.........	8	3
7	" 27	Chicago vs. Louisville	Louisville, Ky....	Chicago...... ..	10	0
8	" 27	Cincin'ti vs. St. Louis	Cincinnati, O......	Cincinnati...	5	2
9	" 29	Louisv'e vs. St. Louis	Louisville, Ky....	St. Louis.......	6	2
10	" 29	Chicago vs. Cincin'ti..	Cincinnati, O.....	Chicago.......	11	5
11	" 29	Boston vs. Hartford...	Boston, Mass.....	Hartford......	3	2
12	May 1	Boston vs. Hartford...	Hartford, Conn...	Hartford	15	3
13	" 2	Athletic vs. Mutual...	Brooklyn, N. Y...	Mutual.........	3	2
14	" 2	Chicago vs. Cincin'ti..	Cincinnati, O......	Chicago.......	15	9
15	" 3	Athletic vs. Mutual...	Philadelphia, Pa.	Athletic......	11	5
16	" 3	Louisv'e vs. St. Louis	Louisville, Ky....	Louisvi le...	11	0
17	" 4	Athletic vs. Mutual...	Philadelphia, Pa.	Athletic......	7	5
18	" 4	Cincin'ti vs. Louisv'e	Cincinnati, O......	Cincinnati...	3	2
19	" 5	Hartford vs. Mutual..	Brooklyn, N. Y...	Hartford......	4	3
20	" 6	Hartford vs. Athletic	Philadelphia, Pa.	Hartford......	6	3
21	" 6	Chicago vs. St. Louis	St. Louis, Mo...	St. Louis......	1	0
22	" 6	Cincin'ti vs. Louisv'e	Cincinnati, O.....	Louisville....	13	8
23	" 6	Boston vs. Mutual.....	Boston, Mass.....	Boston.........	12	3
24	" 8	Athletic vs. Hartford	Philadelphia, Pa.	Hartford......	7	4
25	" 8	Boston vs. Mutual.....	Boston, Mass.....	Mutual.........	5	1
26	" 8	Chicago vs. St. Louis..	St Louis, Mo......	Chicago.......	3	2
27	" 9	Louisv'e vs. St. Louis	St. Louis, Mo......	St. Louis... ..	5	0
28	" 10	Chicago vs. Cincin'ti	Chicago, Ill...	Chicago.......	6	0
29	" 11	Athletic vs. Mutual...	Brooklyn, N. Y...	Athletic.. .	6	5
30	" 11	Chicago vs. Cincin'ti	Chicago, Ill.........	Chicago.......	0	5
31	" 11	Louisv'o vs. St. Louis	St. Louis, Mo......	St. Louis......	3	0
32	" 13	Hartford vs. Mutual..	Hartford, Conn...	Hartford......	23	3
33	" 13	Cincin'ti vs. St. Louis	St. Louis, Mo......	St. Louis......	11	0
34	" 13	Chicago vs. Louisv'e..	Chicago, Ill.........	Chicago.......	4	2
35	" 13	Athletic vs. Boston...	Boston, Mass......	Boston...	19	11
36	" 15	Athletic vs. Boston...	Boston, Mass.....	Boston.........	15	6
37	" 16	Chicago vs. Louisv'e..	Chicago, Ill.........	Chicago.......	4	3
38	" 16	Athletic vs. Hartford	Hartford, Conn...	Hartford......	8	2
39	" 16	Cincin'ti vs. St. Louis	St. Louis, Mo......	St. Louis......	11	1
40	" 17	Boston vs. Hartford...	Boston, Mass......	Hartford......	8	3
41	" 18	Cincin'ti vs. Louisv'e	Louisville, Ky....	Louisville....	9	3
42	" 19	Boston vs. Hartford...	Hartford, Conn...	Hartford......	12	2

RECORD OF CHAMPIONSHIP GAMES—*Continued.*

Number of Games	Date		Names of Contestants	Where Played	Winning Club	Runs Scored	
						Win'g Club	Los'g Club
43	May	19	Chicago vs. St. Louis	Chicago, Ill	St. Louis	4	1
44	"	20	Chicago vs. St. Louis	Chicago, Ill	Chicago	6	3
45	"	20	Cincin'ti vs. Louisv'e	Louisville, Ky	Louisville	3	1
46	"	20	Boston vs. Mutual	Brooklyn, N. Y.	Boston	7	4
47	"	23	St. Louis vs. Mutual	Brooklyn, N. Y.	St. Louis	12	8
48	"	23	Chicago vs. Hartford	Hartford, Conn	Chicago	0	4
49	"	23	Athletic vs. Louisv'e	Philadelphia, Pa	Louisville	3	1
50	"	23	Boston vs. Cincinnati	Boston, Mass	Boston	8	0
51	"	25	Boston vs. Cincinnati	Boston, Mass	Boston	4	0
52	"	25	Mutual vs St. Louis	Brooklyn, N. Y.	St. Louis	2	1
53	"	25	Chicago vs. Hartford	Hartford, Coun	Hartford	4	2
54	"	25	Athletic vs. Louisv'e	Philadelphia, Pa	Tie	2	8
55	"	26	Athletic vs. Louisv'e	Philadelphia, Pa	Louisville	16	0
56	"	27	Athletic vs. Louisv'e	Philadelphia, Pa	Athletic	9	5
57	"	27	Boston vs. Cincinnati	Boston, Mass	Boston	8	1
58	"	27	Chicago vs. Hartford	Hartford, Conn	Chicago	8	2
59	"	27	Mutual vs. St. Louis	Brooklyn, N. Y.	Mutual	6	2
60	"	30	Mutual vs. Louisville	Brooklyn, N. Y.	Mutual	7	0
61	"	30	Cincin'ti vs. Hartford	Hartford, Conn	Hartford	6	1
62	"	30	Boston vs. Chicago	Boston, Mass	Chicago	5	3
63	"	30	Athletic vs. St. Louis	Philadelphia, Pa	St. Louis	7	0
64	June	1	Athletic vs. St. Louis	Philadelphia, Pa	St. Louis	17	3
65	"	1	Boston vs. Chicago	Boston, Mass	Chicago	9	1
66	"	1	Louisville vs. Mutual	Brooklyn, N. Y.	Mutual	5	2
67	"	1	Cincin'ti vs. Hartford	Hartford, Conn	Cincinnati	8	2
68	"	3	Cincin'ti vs. Hartford	Hartford, Conn	Hartford	7	4
69	"	3	Chicago vs. Boston	Boston, Mass	Chicago	8	4
70	"	3	Louisville vs. Mutual	Brooklyn, N. Y.	Louisville	16	11
71	"	3	Athletic vs. St. Louis	Philadelphia, Pa	St. Louis	7	0
72	"	6	Athletic vs. Chicago	Phil'adelphia, Pa	Chicago	3	0
73	"	6	Boston vs. Louisville	Boston, Mass	Louisville	8	4
74	"	6	Hartford vs. St. Louis	Hartford, Conn	Hartford	2	5
75	"	6	Cincin'ti vs. Mutual	Brooklyn, N. Y.	Mutual	21	7
76	"	8	Cincin'ti vs. Mutual	Brooklyn, N Y	Mutual	8	1
77	"	8	Athletic vs. Chicago	Philadelphia, Pa	Chicago	3	5
78	"	8	Boston vs. Louisville	Boston, Mass	Louisville	6	3
79	"	8	Hartford vs St. Louis	Hartford, Conn	Hartford	6	3
80	"	10	Hartford vs. St. Louis	Hartford, Conn	Hartford	4	0
81	"	10	Boston vs. Louisville	Boston, Mass	Louisville	1	4
82	"	10	Cincin'ti vs. Mutual	Brooklyn, N. Y.	Mutual	14	1
83	"	10	Athletic vs Chicago	Philadelphia, Pa	Chicago	5	0
84	"	13	Mutual vs. Chicago	Brooklyn, N. Y.	Chicago	4	6
85	"	13	Hartford vs. Louisv'e	Hartford, Conn	Hartford	20	5
86	"	14	Athletic vs. Cincin'ti	Philadelphia, Pa	Athletic	20	5
87	"	14	Boston vs. St. Louis	Boston, Mass	St. Louis	10	6
88	"	15	Boston vs. St. Louis	Boston, Mass	Boston	11	6
89	"	15	Athletic vs. Cincin'ti	Philadelphia, Pa	Athletic	6	1
90	"	15	Hartford vs Louisv'e	Hartford, Conn	Hartford	6	5
91	"	15	Chicago vs. Mutual	Brooklyn, N. Y.	Mutual	10	3
92	"	17	Chicago vs. Mutual	Brooklyn, N. Y.	Chicago	10	

RECORD OF CHAMPIONSHIP GAMES—*Continued*.

Number of Games	Date	Names of Contestants	Where Played	Winning Club	Win'g Club	Los'g Club
93	June 17	Boston vs. St. Louis	Boston, Mass	St. Louis	12	8
94	"	17 Athletic vs. Cincin'ti	Philadelphia, Pa.	Athletic	23	15
95	"	17 Hartford vs. Louisv'e	Hartford, Conn	Hartford	1	0
96	"	20 Athletic vs. St. Louis	St. Louis, Mo	St. Louis	4	2
97	"	20 Chicago vs. Mutual	Chicago, Ills	Chicago	4	2
98	"	20 Boston vs. Cincinnati	Cincinnati, O	Boston	14	7
99	"	21 Hartford vs. Louisv'e	Louisville, Ky	Tie	5	5
100	"	22 Hartford vs. Louisv'e	Louisville, Ky	Hartford	3	0
101	"	22 Boston vs. Cincinnati	Cincinnati, O	Boston	8	5
102	"	22 Chicago vs. Mutual	Chicago, Ill	Chicago	6	4
103	"	22 Athletic vs. St. Louis	St. Louis, Mo	St. Louis	5	0
104	"	24 Athletic vs. St. Louis	St. Louis, Mo	St. Louis	8	3
105	"	24 Chicago vs. Mutual	Chicago, Ill	Chicago	16	2
106	"	24 Hartford vs. Louisv'e	Louisville, Ky	Louisville	7	2
107	"	24 Boston vs. Cincinnati	Cincinnati, O	Boston	8	7
108	"	26 Hartford vs. Louisv'e	Louisville, Ky	Hartford	3	0
109	"	27 Boston vs. Louisville	Louisville, Ky	Boston	5	3
110	"	27 Cincin'ti vs. Hartford	Cincinnati, O	Hartford	5	2
111	"	27 Mutual vs. St. Louis	St. Louis, Mo	St. Louis	7	1
112	"	27 Athletic vs. Chicago	Chicago, Ill	Athletic	14	13
113	"	29 Athletic vs Chicago	Chicago, Ill	Chicago	19	3
114	"	29 Boston vs. Louisville	Louisville, Ky	Louisville	8	6
115	"	29 Hartford vs. Cincin'ti	Cincinnati, O	Hartford	13	6
116	"	29 Mutual vs. St. Louis	St. Louis, Mo	St. Louis	8	0
117	July 1	Athletic vs. Chicago	Chicago, Ill	Chicago	18	10
118	"	1 Boston vs. Louisville	Louisville, Ky	Boston	10	2
119	"	4 Mutual vs. Louisville	Louisville, Ky	Louisville	4	1
120	"	4 Chicago vs. Hartford	Chicago, Ill	Hartford	3	0
121	"	4 Boston vs. St. Louis	St. Louis, Mo	Boston	4	3
122	"	4 Athletic vs. Cincin'ti	Cincinnati, O	Athletic	6	3
123	"	6 Athletic vs. Cincin'ti	Cincinnati, O	Cincinnati	5	2
124	"	6 Louisville vs. Mutual	Louisville, Ky	Louisville	7	1
125	"	6 Chicago vs. Hartford	Chicago, Ill	Hartford	6	2
126	"	6 Boston vs. St. Louis	St. Louis, Mo	Boston	5	4
127	"	8 Boston vs. St. Louis	St. Louis, Mo	St. Louis	9	5
128	"	8 Chicago vs. Hartford	Chicago, Ill	Chicago	9	3
129	"	8 Louisville vs. Mutual	Louisville, Ky	Tie	5	5
130	"	8 Athletic vs. Cincin'ti	Cincinnati, O	Cincinnati	7	5
131	"	10 Louisville vs. Mutual	Louisville, Ky	Mutual	8	5
132	"	11 Louisv'e vs. Athletic	Louisville, Ky	Louisville	6	2
133	"	11 Cincinnati vs. Mutual	Cincinnati, O	Mutual	8	2
134	"	11 Boston vs. Chicago	Chicago, Ill	Chicago	18	7
135	"	11 Hartford vs. St. Louis	St. Louis, Mo	St. Louis	2	0
136	"	13 Hartford vs. St Louis	St. Louis, Mo	St. Louis	3	0
137	"	13 Boston vs. Chicago	Chicago, Ill	Chicago	11	3
138	"	13 Athletic vs. Louisv'e	Louisville, Ky	Louisville	11	5
139	"	13 Cincin'ti vs. Mutual	Cincinnati, O	Mutual	13	8
140	"	15 Cincin'ti vs. Mutual	Cincinnati, O	Mutual	8	6
141	"	15 Hartford vs St. Louis	St. Louis, Mo	St. Louis	2	0
142	"	15 Boston vs Chicago	Chicago, Ill	Chicago	15	0

RECORD OF CHAMPIONSHIP GAMES—*Continued.*

Number of Games	Date	Names of Contestants.	Where Played.	Winning Club.	Win'g Club.	Los'g Club.
143	July	15 Athletic vs. Louisv'e.	Louisville. Ky....	Athletic......	8	5
144	"	18 Chicago vs. Louisv'e..	Chicago, Ill........	Chicago......	9	5
145	"	18 Cincin'ti vs. St. Louis	St. Louis, Mo......	St. Louis.....	5	1
146	"	19 Athletic vs. Boston...	Philadelphia, Pa.	Boston..........	10	7
147	"	20 Mutual vs. Boston....	Brooklyn, N. Y..	Boston........	7	1
148	"	20 Chicago vs. Louisv'e.	Chicago, Ill........	Chicago.......	18	0
149	"	20 Cincin'ti vs. St. Louis	Cincinnati, O.....	St. Louis......	9	1
150	"	21 Athletic vs. Hartford	Philadelphia, Pa.	Hartford......	6	4
151	"	22 Chicago vs. Louisv'e	Chicago, Ill........	Chicago.......	30	7
152	"	22 Hartford vs. Mutual..	Brooklyn, N. Y..	Mutual.......	7	3
153	"	22 Cincin'ti vs. St. Louis	St. Louis, Mo......	St. Louis....	5	1
154	"	25 Cincin'ti vs. Chicago.	Chicago, Ill........	Chicago.......	23	3
155	"	25 Boston vs. Mutual.....	Boston, Mass......	Boston........	11	1
156	"	25 Louisv'e vs. St. Louis	St. Louis, Mo.....	Louisville....	7	4
157	"	27 Louisv'e vs. St. Louis	St. Louis, Mo......	Louisville....	4	2
158	"	27 Chicago vs. Cincin'ti.	Chicago, Ill........	Chicago.......	17	3
159	"	27 Boston vs. Mutual.....	Boston, Mass......	Boston........	18	6
160	"	29 Boston vs. Mutual.....	Boston, Mass......	Boston........	17	8
161	"	29 Chicago vs. Cincin'ti.	Chicago, Ill........	Chicago.......	9	2
162	"	29 Louisv'e vs. St. Louis	St. Louis, Mo	St. Louis......	7	0
163	Aug.	1 Cincin'ti vs. St. Louis	Cincinnati, O......	St. Louis......	19	3
164	"	1 Chicago vs. Louisv'e..	Louisville, Ky...	Chicago......	16	7
165	"	1 Athletic vs. Hartford	Hartford, Conn...	Hartford......	8	4
166	"	2 Athletic vs. Hartford	Hartford, Conn...	Hartford......	15	5
167	"	3 Athletic vs. Boston...	Boston, Mass......	Boston.........	8	3
168	"	8 Cincin d vs. St. Louis	Cincinnati, O......	St. Louis......	10	0
169	"	8 Boston vs. Athletic...	Boston, Mass......	Boston........	13	6
170	"	8 Hartford vs. Mutual..	Hartford, Conn...	Mutual.......	4	1
171	"	8 Chicago vs. Louisville	Louisville, Ky....	Louisville....	9	2
172	"	7 Chicago vs. Louisville	Louisville, Ky....	Chicago.......	0	3
173	"	7 Athletic vs. Boston...	Boston, Mass......	Boston........	6	5
174	"	7 Hartford vs. Mutual..	Hartford, Conn...	Mutual.	2	1
175	"	8 Hartford vs. Athletic.	Hartford, Conn...	Hartford......	3	1
176	"	8 Chicago vs. Cincin ti.	Cincinnati, O......	Chicago.......	13	3
177	"	8 Louisv'e vs. St. Louis	Louisville, Ky...	St. Louis......	3	0
178	"	9 Athletic vs. Hartford	Hartford, Conn...	Hartford......	9	1
179	"	10 Athletic vs. Mutual...	Brooklyn, N. Y...	Mutual.......	9	7
180	"	10 Louisv'e vs. St. Louis	Louisville, Ky...	Louisville...	4	2
181	"	10 Chicago vs. Cincin'ti.	Cincinnati, O......	Chicago.......	6	4
182	"	11 Hartford vs. Mutual..	Brooklyn, N. Y...	Hartford......	14	11
183	"	12 Hartford vs. Athletic	Philadelphia, Pa.	Athletic......	15	0
184	"	12 Chicago vs. Cincin'ti.	Cincinnati, O......	Chicago.......	5	2
185	"	12 Louisv'e vs. St. Louis	Louisville, Ky...	St. Louis......	5	4
186	"	14 Athletic vs. Hartford	Philadelphia, Pa.	Hartford....	6	3
187	"	15 Chicago vs. St. Louis.	St. Louis, Mo......	St. Louis....	17	5
188	"	15 Cincin'ti vs. Louisv'e	Louisville, Ky....	Louisville....	3	0
189	"	17 Chicago vs. St. Louis.	St. Louis, Mo......	St. Louis....	13	5
190	"	17 Athletic vs. Mutual...	Philadelphia, Pa.	Athletic......	4	1
191	"	18 Cincin'ti vs. Louisv'e	Louisville, Ky....	Louisville....	4	4
192	"	18 Boston vs. Hartford...	Boston, Mass......	Hartford....	5	4

RECORD OF CHAMPIONSHIP GAMES—Continued.

Number of Games	Date	Names of Contestants	Where Played	Winning Club	Win'g Club	Los'g Club
103	Aug.	19 Boston vs. Hartford...	Boston, Mass......	Boston........	13	4
104	"	19 Athletic vs. Mutual...	Philadelphia, Pa.	Mutual........	17	9
195	"	19 Cincin'ti vs. Louisv'e	Louisville, Ky....	Louisville....	6	3
196	"	21 Boston vs. Hartford ..	Hartford, Conn..	Hartford... ..	10	4
197	"	21 Chicago vs. St. Louis.	St. Louis, Mo......	St. L Forf'd.	7	6
198	"	22 Chicago vs. St. Louis.	Chicago, Ill........	Chicago.......	12	2
199	"	22 Cincin'ti vs. Louisv'e.	Cincinnati, O......	Lo'isville....	8	0
200	"	22 Boston vs. Hartford....	Hartford, Conn...	Boston........	6	5
201	"	23 Boston vs. Athletic...	Philadelphia, Pa.	Boston........	7	6
202	"	24 Boston vs. Athletic...	Philadelphia, Pa.	Boston........	11	6
203	"	25 Boston vs. Mutual.....	Brooklyn, N. Y...	Boston........	15	4
204	"	25 Cincin'ti vs. Louisv'e.	Cincinnati, O......	Cincinnati...	3	1
205	"	25 Chicago vs. St. Louis.	Chicago, Ill........	St. Louis.....	8	6
206	"	26 Chicago vs. St. Louis.	Chicago, Ill........	Chicago.......	23	3
207	"	26 Boston vs. Mutual.....	Brooklyn, N. Y...	Mutual.......	10	9
208	"	26 Cincin'ti vs. Louisv'e	Cincinnati, O......	Louisville....	3	2
209	Sept.	5 Athletic vs. Chicago..	Philadelphia, Pa.	Chicago......	11	5
210	"	5 Mutual vs. St. Louis..	Brooklyn, N. Y...	St. Louis.....	9	0
211	"	5 Hartford vs. Louisv'e	Hartford, Conn...	Hartford	6	1
212	"	5 Boston vs. Cincinnati	Boston, Mass......	Boston........	17	4
213	"	6 Boston vs. Cincinnati	Boston, Mass......	Boston........	7	3
214	"	6 Athletic vs. Chicago..	Philadelphia, Pa.	Chicago.......	15	3
215	"	6 Mutual vs. St. Louis..	Brooklyn, N. Y...	St. Louis.....	4	3
216	"	6 Hartford vs. Louisv'e	Hartford, Conn...	Hartford	6	3
217	"	8 Boston vs. Louisville	Boston, Mass......	Boston	6	3
218	"	8 Athletic vs. St. Louis	Philadelphia, Pa.	St. Louis.....	20	5
219	"	8 Chicago vs. Mutual...	Brooklyn, N. Y...	Chicago.......	16	0
220	"	9 Chicago vs. Mutual...	Brooklyn, N. Y...	Chicago.......	13	4
221	"	9 Athletic vs. St. Louis	Philadelphia, Pa.	St. Louis.....	15	2
222	" 9 AM	Cincin'ti vs. Hartford	Cincinnati, Conn...	Hartford......	14	4
223	" 3PM	Cincin'ti vs. Hartford	Hartford, Conn..	Hartford.....	8	4
224	"	11 Boston vs. Louisville	Boston, Mass......	Boston........	8	0
225	"	12 Chicago vs. Hartford.	Hartford, Conn..	Hartford......	8	7
226	"	12 Boston vs. St. Louis..	Boston, Mass......	St. Louis.....	5	2
227	"	12 Louisville vs. Mutual	Brooklyn, N. Y...	Louisville....	7	4
228	"	12 Athletic vs. Cincin'ti.	Philadelphia, Pa.	Athletic	12	3
229	"	13 Athletic vs. Cincin'ti.	Philadelphia, Pa.	Cincinnati...	15	13
230	"	13 Chicago vs. Hartford.	Hartford, Conn...	Chicago.......	6	2
231	"	13 Boston vs. St. Louis...	Boston, Mass......	Boston.......	0	5
232	"	13 Louisville vs. Mutual	Brooklyn, N. Y...	Louisville....	9	4
233	"	15 Cincinnati vs. Mutual	Brooklyn, N. Y...	Mutual.......	2	1
234	"	15 Chicago vs. Boston....	Boston, Mass......	Chicago.......	9	3
235	"	15 Hartford vs. St. Louis	Hartford, Conn...	St. Louis.....	6	2
236	"	15 Athletic vs. Louisv'e.	Philad-lphia, Pa.	Louisville....	3	0
237	"	16 Athletic vs. Louisv'e.	Philadelphia, Pa.	Louisville....	7	6
238	"	16 Cincin'ti vs. Mutual..	Brooklyn, N. Y...	Cincinnati...	0	6
239	"	16 Hartford vs. St. Louis	Hartford, Conn...	St. Louis.....	6	4
240	"	16 Boston vs. Chicago ...	Boston, Mass......	Chicago......	7	2
241	"	22 Boston vs. Chicago ...	Chicago, Ill........	Chicago......	12	10
242	"	23 Boston vs. Chicago ...	Chicago, Ill........	Boston........	10	9

Number of Games.	Date.	Names of Contestants.	Where Played.	Winning Club.	Runs Scored. Win'g Club.	Runs Scored. Los'g Club.
243	Sept.	26 Hartford vs. Chicago	Chicago, Ill........	Chicago........	7	6
244	"	27 Hartford vs. Chicago	Chicago, Ill........	Chicago........	16	10
245	"	27 Boston vs. Cincinnati	Cincinnati, O.....	Boston.........	5	3
246	"	28 Boston vs. Cincinnati	Cincinnati, O.....	Boston........	10	7
247	"	29 Boston vs. Louisville	Louisville, Ky....	Louisville....	3	0
248	"	29 Hartford vs. St. Louis	St. Louis, Mo......	St. Louis	5	2
249	"	30 Hartford vs. St. Louis	St. Louis, Mo......	Hartford......	4	1
250	"	30 Boston vs. Louisville	Louisville, Ky....	Boston........	6	5
251	Oct.	3 Boston vs. St. Louis...	St. Louis, Mo......	St. Louis......	5	3
252	"	4 Boston vs. St. Louis...	St. Louis, Mo......	St. Louis......	3	2
253	"	4 Hartford vs. Louisv'e	Louisville, Ky....	Hartford......	6	0
254	"	5 Hartford vs. Louisv'e	Louisville, Ky....	Hartford......	11	2
255	"	6 Hartford vs. Cincin'ti	Cincinnati, O.....	Hartford	7	4
256	"	7 Hartford vs. Cincin'ti	Cincinnati, O.....	Hartford	11	6
257	"	9 Hartford vs. Cincin'ti	Cincinnati, O.....	Hartford	11	0
258	"	17 Hartford vs. Mutual..	Brooklyn, N. Y..	Hartford	3	0
259	"	20 Hartford vs. Boston..	Boston, Mass......	Hartford	5	0
260	"	21 Hartford vs. Boston..	Boston, Mass......	Hartford	11	1

TOTAL NUMBER OF RUNS SCORED, 3,066.

RUNS SCORED BY CLUBS.

Chicago	624	Opponents	257
Hartford	429	Opponents	261
St. Louis	386	Opponents	229
Boston	471	Opponents	450
Louisville	280	Opponents	344
Mutual	260	Opponents	412
Athletic	378	Opponents	534
Cincinnati	238	Opponents	579
Total	3,066		3,066

Average number of Runs scored per Game by winning Clubs, 8.59.
Average number of Runs scored per Game by losing Clubs, 3.20.

The following is an official list of the Officers and Players of Clubs belonging to the "National League of Professional Base Ball Clubs," for the season of 1877 (as far as completed to January 18, 1877).

BOSTON B. B. C. of BOSTON, MASS.

HARRY WRIGHT, *Sec'y and Manager, No. 39 Eliot St.*

George Wright.	H. C. Shafer.
A. J. Leonard.	John Manning.
James Rourk.	T. Murnan.
John Morrill.	James White.
L. Brown.	Thomas II. Bond.
W. E. White.	E. B. Sutton.

CHICAGO BALL CLUB, of CHICAGO, ILL.

W. A. HULBERT, *President.*   A. G. SPALDING, *Secretary.*
Room 4, No. 166 Randolph St.

A. G. Spalding.	C. C. Waitt,
R. C. Barnes.	J. P. Peters.
C. A. McVey.	J. W. Glenn.
P. A. Hines.	G. W. Bradley.
A. C. Anson.	Harry W. Smith.

CINCINNATI B. B. C., of CINCINNATI, O.

J. L. KECK, *President, No. 80 Poplar St.*
C. W. Jones.

Henry Kessler.	W. B. Foley.
N. W. Hicks.	Robert Mathews.
James Hallinan.	A. S. Booth.
Lipman Pike.	Robert E. Addy.

HARTFORD B. B. C., of HARTFORD, CONN.

M. G. BULKELEY, *President.*   H. L. BUNCE, *Secretary.*

Robert Ferguson.	Thomas Carey.
J. J. Burdock.	W. A. Harbidge.
Thomas York.	James Holdsworth.
Joseph Start.	John C. Cassidy.

D. Allison.

LOUISVILLE B. B. C., of LOUISVILLE, KY.

W. N. HALDEMAN, *Pres't.*   C. E. CHASE, *Vice Pres't,*
No. 12 Third St.
SAMUEL CASSEDAY, Jr., *Sec'y.*   JOHN C. CHAPMAN, *Manager.*

James A. Devlin.	Charles Snyder.
W. L. Hague.	John J. Ryan.

Joseph J. Gerhardt.

ST. LOUIS B. B. C., of ST. LOUIS, MO.

J. B. C. Lucas, *Pres't.*   Chas. H. Turner, *Treas.*
C. O. Bishop, *Vice Pres't.*   Charles A. Fowle, *Sec'y,*
George McManus, *Manager,* 820 North 6th Street.

John E. Clapp.	H. J. Dehlman.
Joseph V. Battin.	J. J. Remsen.
F. C. Nichols.	J. W. Blong.
D. W. Force.	M. H. McGeary.
M. C. Dorgan.	Arthur F. Croft.

Extract from the minutes of the "League," held in Cleveland, O., December 7, 1876:

"*Resolved,* That the publication of the Official Book be left in the hands of the Secretary."

By the authority vested in me, by virtue of the above resolution, I hereby certify that Messrs. A. G. Spalding & Bro., of Chicago, Ill., have been granted the *exclusive* right to publish the Official Book for 1877.

N. E. YOUNG, *Secretary.*

FAIRBANKS' BASE BALL CLUB,

SOLE LESSEES

WHITE STOCKING BASE BALL PARK,

CHICAGO, ILLINOIS.

U A. FORSYTH, President.   E. C. DURFEE, Vice President.
B. F. STANGLAND, Secretary.   G. J. HADLEY, Manager.

The Fairbanks Club is the leading Amateur Club of Chicago, and has rented the grounds of the Chicago Ball Club for the season of 1877, thus securing control of the only enclosed ball ground in Chicago.

Semi-professional and Amateur Clubs visiting this vicinity and desiring to play in Chicago, will please address   A. O. KELLOGG,
111 and 113 Lake St., Chicago, Ill.

THE CHICAGO TRIBUNE.

THE WESTERN BASE BALL AUTHORITY.

THE SUNDAY EDITION

OF THE

CHICAGO TRIBUNE

Contains more and better prepared news from the National Game and from other sports than any other daily paper published in the United States.

During 1877, THE TRIBUNE will continue its full telegraphic reports of all Championship Games, together with interesting correspondence from all quarters.

Every club and club-room should keep THE SUNDAY TRIBUNE on file.

TERMS:

SUNDAY EDITION, 16 Pages, per year, - - - - $2.50
DAILY TRIBUNE, including Sunday, - - - . 14.50

Address

THE TRIBUNE,

Chicago, Illinois.

Chicago, Milwaukee & St. Paul R'y.

THE GREAT THROUGH LINE.

CHICAGO---NORTHWEST,

Wisconsin, Northern Iowa,

Minnesota, Dakota, Manitoba,

AND THE BLACK HILLS,

Passing through a finer country, with grander scenery, and connecting more business centers and pleasure resorts than any other Northwestern Line.

Connecting in

Chicago with all Eastern and Southern Lines.

Chicago Depot, Corner Canal and West Madison Streets.

Horse Cars and Stage Lines for all parts of the city constantly passing.

CHICAGO CITY OFFICE, 61 and 63 CLARK ST.

THE ONLY THROUGH LINE BETWEEN

Chicago, Milwaukee, Sparta, La Crosse, Winona,

Madison, McGregor, Owatonna, St. Paul and Minneapolis,

Traversing the Valley of the Upper Mississippi River, and along the shore of Lake Pepin, and through Northern Iowa and Central Minnesota.

Base Ball Clubs, Theatrical Companies, and Minstrel Troupes, please "BOOK IT," that this is the route for them to travel in order to reach MORE AND BETTER PAYING POINTS than can be done by any other Northwestern line.

Palace Sleeping Cars and Day Coaches, with Westinghouse's improved Automatic Air Brake, on all through trains.

A. V. H. CARPENTER,

Gen. Pass. and Ticket Agent.

LEAGUE HOTELS.

The following hotels are patronized by all League Clubs, and are recognized as the base ball headquarters in their respective cities. Special rates are given, and the best of accommodation provided.

Letters addressed to traveling clubs in care of any of the following hotels will be very apt to reach their destination.

SPECIAL NOTICE.

We now manufacture nearly everything in the Base Ball line, and are better enabled to warrant our goods than heretofore, and everything we offer may be relied upon as the best in the market. Being practical ball players, we are enabled to anticipate the wants of our patrons, and select our stock accordingly, and, as we deal *directly* with players, have to keep the very best of everything.

CATCHERS' GLOVES.

We have an excellent stock of catchers' gloves, well padded and good style, at the following prices:

Per Pair.

No. 1, Medium Quality, well padded.........................$1.00
" 2, First   "   "   " 1.50
" 3, Extra   ".   Indian tanned buck................. 2.50

Sent by mail upon receipt of price.
BASES, BAT BAGS, MARBLE and IRON HOME PLATES always in stock.

BOXING GLOVES.

We would call the attention of the lovers of the art of boxing to our stock of Gloves. They are of the best workmanship, well stuffed and sewed, and we have the largest and most complete assortment in the West.

	Per Set.		Per Set.
No. 0, Boys' size,	$3.50	No. 3½ Heel Padded......	5.50
" 1, Men's "	4.00	" 4,......................	6.00
" 2,	4.50	" 4½, Heel Padded.....	6.50
" 3,	5.00	" 5, White Kid..........	7.00

Address   A. G. SPALDING & BRO.,
118 Randolph St.,
ustrated Catalogue free.   CHICAGO, ILL.